FOCUS ON EVANGELISM

FOCUS ON EVANGELISM

READINGS FOR THINKING IT THROUGH

EDITED BY
GEORGE HUNTER

Discipleship Resources
Nashville

FOCUS ON EVANGELISM. © 1978 by Discipleship Resources. All rights reserved. Printed in the United States of America. No part of this book may be used or reproduced in any manner whatsoever without written permission except in the case of brief quotations embodied in critical articles and reviews. For information address Discipleship Resources, P. O. Box 840, Nashville, Tennessee 37202.

EV070B

CONTENTS

INTRODUCTION

PART ONE: FOCUS FROM THEOLOGY

1. What Is Evangelism?   13
   James I. Packer

2. Methods and Strategy in the Evangelism of the Early Church   26
   Michael Green

3. Conversion   40
   Stephen C. Neill

4. The New Birth   49
   L. Harold DeWolf

5. The Highest Priority: Cross-Cultural Evangelism   59
   Ralph D. Winter

PART TWO: FOCUS UPON PRACTICE

6. The Setting for Making Christians Today   71
   Donald Soper

7. What Is the Matter with Preaching?   79
   Harry Emerson Fosdick

8. An Outline of the Principles of Evangelistic Preaching   90
   Lawrence L. Lacour

9. Would Jesus Stoop to Canned Evangelism?   97
   Tom Hanks

10. The Art of Communication   101
    Bruce Larson

11. Counseling the Seeker   108
    Canon Bryan Green

12. Let's March Abreast: the Congregation in Evangelism   125
    George E. Sweazey

ABOUT THE WRITERS...

J. I. Packer, British theologian, and author of *Evangelism and the Sovereignty of God.*

Michael Green, biblical scholar and pastor-evangelist of the Anglican Church adjacent to Oxford University. Author of *Evangelism in the Early Church, New Life—New Lifestyle,* and *I Believe in the Holy Spirit.*

Stephen C. Neill, Anglican missionary statesman and historian, author of *A History of Christian Missions, Call to Mission,* and *Salvation Tomorrow.*

L. Harold DeWolf, systematic theologian and Dean-emeritus of Wesley Theological Seminary, author of *A Theology of the Living Church* and *Responsible Freedom.*

Ralph D. Winter, missionary historian, now Director of the Center for World Evangelization.

Donald Soper, British open-air soap-box adovcate, life-peer in The House of Lords, and author of *The Advocacy of the Gospel* and *Tower Hill 12:30.*

Harry Emerson Fosdick, late pastor of Riverside Church, New York City and Professor of Homiletics at Union Theological Seminary, author of *The Power to See It Through* and *A Great Time to Be Alive.*

Lawrence L. Lacour, former pastor of First United Methodist Church of Colorado Springs, Colorado, widely traveled evangelist, now Professor of Preaching at Oral Roberts University School of Theology.

Tom Hanks, para-church leader in evangelism and related ministries, frequent contributor to religious periodicals.

Bruce Larson, Presbyterian clergyman, former Director of Faith-At-Work, widely read author.

Bryan Green, widely traveled Anglican evangelist and rector of Birmingham, England for twenty-two years, author of *The Practice of Evangelism* and *Saints Alive.*

George E. Sweazey, former secretary for evangelism for the United Presbyterian Church in the U.S.A., and professor of preaching and evangelism at Princeton Theological Seminary, author of *Effective Evangelism, Preaching the Good News* and *The Congregation as Evangelist.*

PERMISSIONS

"What Is Evangelism?" by James I. Packer. From *Theological Perspectives on Church Growth*, Harvie M. Conn, ed., Presbyterian & Reformed Publishing Company, 1976. Used by permission of Presbyterian & Reformed Company, P.O. Box 817, Phillipsburg, New Jersey 08865.

"Would Jesus Stoop to Canned Evangelism?". From *Eternity*, September 1973. Used by permission of ETERNITY Magazine. Copyright 1973 by Evangelical Ministries, 1716 Spruce Street, Philadelphia, Pennsylvania 19103.

"Let's March Abreast" by George E. Sweazey. From *Evangelism Now*, Ralph G. Turnbull, ed., Baker Book House, 1972. Copyright 1972 by Baker Book House. Used by permission.

"What Is the Matter with Preaching?" by Harry Emerson Fosdick. Copyright 1928 by *Harper's Magazine*. Copyright renewed 1956. All rights reserved. Reprinted from the July 1928 issue by special permission.

"The Setting for Making Christians Today" by Donald Soper. From *The Advocacy of the Gospel*, Donald Soper, Hodder and Stoughton, 1961. Copyright 1961 by Donald Soper. Used by permission of Hodder & Stoughton Limited, 47 Bedford Square, London WC1B 3DP, England.

"Counseling the Seeker" by Bryan Green. Reprinted by permission of Charles Scribner's Sons from THE PRACTICE OF EVANGELISM by Bryan Green. Copyright 1951 Charles Scribner's Sons.

"Conversion" by Bishop Stephen C. Neill, From *The Scottish Journal of Theology*, Vol. III, 1950. Used by permission.

"An Outline of the Principles of Evangelistic Preaching" by Lawrence L. Lacour. Used by permission of Discipleship Resources.

"The Art of Communication" by Bruce Larson. From SETTING MEN FREE by Bruce Larson. Copyright 1967 by Zondervan Publishing House. Used by permission.

"Methods and Strategy in the Evangelization of the Early Church" by Michael Green. From LET THE EARTH HEAR HIS VOICE. Copyright 1975 by World Wide Publications. Used by permission.

"The New Birth" by L. Harold DeWolf. From A THEOLOGY OF THE LIVING CHURCH, Chapter 34, by L. Harold DeWolf. Copyright 1953 by Harper & Row, Publishers, Inc. Reprinted by permission of the publishers.

"The Highest Priority: Cross-Cultural Evangelism" by Ralph D. Winter. Reprinted by permission from *Mission Trends No. 2*, "Evangelization," edited by Gerald H. Anderson and Thomas F. Stransky (New York: Paulist Press; and Grand Rapids, Michigan: William B. Eerdmans Publishing Co. © 1975). Full text appeared originally in LET THE EARTH HEAR HIS VOICE, © 1975 by World Wide Publications.

INTRODUCTION

Some church leaders, preparing for the outreach of their congregation to undiscipled people, want and expect a prescribed method for evangelizing. There are many such prescribed methods now available, and, as the Tom Hanks article in this book acknowledges, the best of them make a definite contribution.

Some church leaders do *not* want a "canned" prescription approach, but want to think it through for themselves—not in abstraction, but bouncing off of good representative literature and models. This book is intended for this second large audience, and provides some of the best resources available in the English language for helping a church's leaders to "think it through."

These readings are pulled from many sources not readily attainable for most church leaders—such as a book long out of print, or a periodical not usually found in one's average town library (such as *The Scottish Journal of Theology*). Several of these entries are now classics. Several focus on an issue more clearly than anyone else ever has. Several present the results of extensive research in an unusually digestible form. Several are very widely influential, several others deserve to be. Every reading has been extensively used by the editor with many groups of lay people and pastors, so their usefulness is field tested and proven.

Most major topics in contemporary evangelization are addressed by one or another of these entries. In Part One, articles will help the reader: to adequately define evangelism and consider its message; to perceive its foundations in the mission of the apostolic church; to clarify evangelism's role in enabling conversion and new birth; and to consider contemporary evangelism's most neglected dimension.

In Part Two, after a classic statement regarding today's secular setting for the ministry of evangelism, the reader will be enabled to consider the roles of evangelistic proclamation, witness, and counseling, and the organizing of the congregation for programmatic outreach.

I offer these resources for the purpose stated above, but with several accompanying pleas. Do not let this be a mere intellectual exercise, or the kind of escapist behavior revealed in many churchmen who are "not yet" actually reaching out because they are in their (say) eighth year of defining "evangelism." Avoid like the plague this debilitating paralysis of analysis. "The harvest is great" in America today, and many "lost" people are receptive, searching, trying everything from astrology to Zen, and are waiting to be "found" by Christ's holy flock and brought as new disciples into his fold.

So, don't wait until you have everything straight and all of your questions answered before your church reaches out. Besides, much that you learn about "how to evangelize" will come not before your attempts at outreach but during such attempts, and in prayerful reflection after. Above all, do not neglect that empowerment promised by the same Spirit who is now preparing people in the world to hear the Great News and to receive Him and the life of the kingdom.

George Hunter

PART ONE:
FOCUS FROM THEOLOGY

1.
WHAT IS EVANGELISM?
JAMES I. PACKER

"Most evangelists," writes Michael Green, "are not very interested in theology: most theologians are not very interested in evangelism."[1] This testimony, alas, is true. Evangelism and theology for the most part go separate ways, and the result is great loss for both. When theology is not held on course by the demands of evangelistic communication, it grows abstract and speculative, wayward in method, theoretical in interest and irresponsible in stance. When evangelism is not fertilized, fed and controlled by theology, it becomes a stylized performance seeking its effect through manipulative skills rather than the power of vision and the force of truth. Both theology and evangelism are then, in one important sense, unreal, false to their own God-given nature; for all true theology has an evangelistic thrust, and all true evangelism is theology in action. That this double unreality exists today needs no proof to me. Seventy years ago, a generation after evangelism and theology had parted company in Scotland, James Denney pleaded for a reuniting of the two interests. "If evangelists were our theologians or theologians our evangelists, we should be nearer the ideal," he wrote; for "the evangelist is in the last resort the judge of theology. If it does not serve his purpose it is not true." For himself, he declared, "I haven't the faintest interest in any theology which doesn't help us to evangelize."[2] But Denney's words went unheeded, and the separation of theology and evangelism remains a characteristic fact of the late twentieth-century world.

It has been a fact of unhappy consequence for evangelism in several ways. First, it has led to evangelism being equated with revivalist procedures, or, at any rate, revivalism being regarded as evangelism *par excellence*. The revivalist pattern, with its special meetings and preachers, its aura of romance and excitement, its claims to supreme spiritual importance, and its methods and techniques for "drawing in the net" was created by such men as the "new school" Pelagian, Charles G. Finney,[3] and that much-loved exponent of the "simple gospel," Dwight L. Moody.[4] That God has worked, and worked wonderfully, through men who have used this pattern is undoubted, but one can still ask whether he has done so because of, or despite, this or that feature of it. Unfortunately, however, there is no agreed answer to such questions, for evangelical theology has done so little to evaluate the revivalist pattern in a theologically disciplined way. Pietistic and revivalist norms of "gospel preaching" and Christian conversion have tended either to be accepted uncritically or to be criticized undiscerningly. Revivalism has come under the hammer often enough from sacramentalist, liberal, radical and secularist standpoints, but these critiques, being shaped by doubts as to whether a definite conversion experience is valid or valuable, have not helped evangelicals who see this experience as biblical, beneficial and a privilege to assess what they say and do to induce it. Puffs for revivalism and squibs against it have come from evangelical sources, but little more; and meantime the updated revivalism of Dr. Billy Graham's crusades and organization continues as the greatest single force (so it would seem to the casual observer) in evangelism today.

Through revivalist crusades, and smaller ventures modelled on them, men and women are finding salvation, and for this one thanks God. Yet it cannot be denied that the situation as described has its problems. To his own embarrassment, the evangelist finds himself regarded as a nobler and wiser person than any theologian and his methods viewed as a kind of sacred cow, which none may touch and against which none may speak. Also, those who evangelize by other than revivalist means (e.g., through the structures of Christian nurture in church and home) find themselves constantly under suspicion of neither understanding nor practicing evangelism at all. Also, such discussions of evangelism as arise under the shadow of revivalism regularly center upon the methods to employ rather than the message to convey; and this is most unhelpful, because it is in connection with the message that the deepest disagreements about evangelism emerge. For if you are (say) a universalist, construing the gospel as a call to wake up to the fact that we are all in a saved state; or a Tillichian, understanding "God" as the name for whatever is our "ultimate concern," or an old-style liberal, for whom the good news is that we are God's children by nature and can never be anything else; or one who thinks that to join the visible church is to enter the sphere of actual salvation automatically—then your evangelistic message, to which you invite response, will be significantly different from that of the man for whom the gospel is God's call to sinners to turn to Christ, for shelter from the wrath to come (cf. 1 Thess. 1:9f.). To argue about methods while agreement on the message is lacking is inept; but revivalism, with its stress on techniques, has unfortunately encouraged this kind of ineptness.

The confusions indicated above have been augmented in recent years by the radical reconceiving of evangelism to which, as it seems, the World Council of Churches has now given its blessing.[5] Rejecting as paternalistic all idea of "propaganda" and "proselytizing"—that is, of making disciples and planting new churches—this novel concept identifies the church's evangelistic task as one of exhibiting the *shalom* (peace, harmony, human community, integrity and justice) which Jesus brought into the world, and of laboring to extend it where it is lacking. Evangelism thus ceases to be primarily a matter of speaking and becomes instead primarily a matter of practicing a serving presence among men. The true task of mission (it is said) is one of "entering into partnership with God in history to renew society,"[6] and for this task the world must be allowed to write the agenda. In this context of a humanizing commitment, dialogue with men of other faiths and of no faith will certainly occur, but its aim will be to achieve mutual understanding and respect within the bonds of our common manhood rather than to persuade anyone to become a Christian. Thus evangelism is radically secularized. As C. Peter Wagner correctly puts it: "Whatever good works the church does, become evangelism, according to this definition. Harvey Cox says, for example, 'Any distinction between social action and evangelism is a mistaken one' . . . . This is 'presence evangelism.' A silent Christian presence, characterized by good works and charity, is called 'evangelism.' "[7] This is as far as possible from the revivalist idea of evangelism as the attempt to induce one-by-one personal conversion. One understands the desire of ecumenical missionary strategists to avoid giving any impression among the younger nations of ideological imperialism, and one applauds all who for Christ's sake seek to humanize a brutal and oppressive world; but one still has to ask, is there any correspondence between this essentially non-communicative program and *evangelism*, as the Bible presents it? If revivalist evangelism needs a little correction from Scripture, surely radical evangelism needs far, far more.

The Concept of Evangelism

If, now, we turn to the Bible and allow it to instruct us, we find that it yields a concept of evangelism that is Trinitarian and theocentric. Evangelism is usually defined as man's work, and this man-centeredness leads to many mistakes about it; but the basic biblical perspective is that evangelism is *a work of God.* God the creator, in the glory and power of his tri-unity, is both God the redeemer and God the evangelist. God's world lies under judgment because of mankind's apostasy and sin; "the wrath of God is revealed from heaven against all ungodliness and unrighteousness of men, who suppress the truth in unrighteousness" (Rom. 1:18). But God loves the world to which, because of sin, he is hostile; "God so loved the world, that he gave his only begotten Son, that whoever believes in him should not perish, but have eternal life" (John 3:16). He is the God who in love *sends.* The Father "loved us and sent his Son to be the propitiation for our sins" (I John 4:10); the Son brought us knowledge of the Father (John 14:9); now the Father and the Son have sent the Spirit to testify and give knowledge of the Son (John 14:26; 15:26; 16:14), and of his Father as our Father through him (cf. John 20:17). It is through the Spirit's agency that blind eyes and hard hearts are opened, so that Christ is acknowledged in his divine glory as our savior and Lord. "God, who said, 'Light shall shine out of darkness,' is the One who has shone in our hearts, to give the light of the knowledge of the glory of God in the face of Christ" (II Cor. 4:6). "No one can say, 'Jesus is Lord,' except by the Holy

Spirit" (I Cor. 12:3)—but when the Spirit enlightens, this is precisely what men do say. Thus God in sovereign love overcomes the spiritual paralysis and perversity of the fallen human heart, and through this inward teaching by the Spirit draws us to himself (John 6:44 f., cf. I John 2:27). "If one may employ an anthropopathism and ascribe human feelings to God," wrote R. B. Kuiper—and surely he was right to think that one may—"God has a passion for souls,"[8] and this is how God expresses and satisfies it. He made us; he loved us; he ransoms us; he reclaims us. "Salvation is from the Lord" (Jonah 2:9).

But this is not the whole story. In the Bible evangelism is not only a work of God, it is also a work of man or rather *a work of God through man*. As God sent his Son to become man and so to "explain" him (cf. John 1:18), so now, adhering to the incarnational principle, if we may so speak, he sends Christian men to be heralds, ambassadors and teachers in His name and on His behalf. (These are the three main words that Paul uses to express his office as God's spokesman κηρυξ, πρεσβυς, διδασκαλος.) The task which God gives to his messengers is primarily and essentially one of proclamation, which the New Testament expresses chiefly by the use of three verbs with their cognate nouns: ευαγγελιζομαι (tell the good news, ευαγγελιον); κηρυσσω (utter an announcement, κηρυγμα), and μαρτυρεω (bear witness, μαρτυρια). The proclamation is not, however, to be made on a casual, take-it-or-leave-it basis; the end in view is to "persuade" (πειθω, II Cor. 5:11 etc.), to "disciple" (μαθητευω, Acts 14:21), and so to "turn" or "convert" επιστρεφω verb which in this sense is used with the evangelist or the sinner, not God, as its subject, as when Paul tells Agrippa that Christ sent him to the Gentiles "to open their eyes so that they may turn (or, to turn them) from darkness to light" (Acts 26:18, cf. Luke 1:16; James 5:19f.). Evangelism, as I wrote elsewhere, is "communication with a view to conversion."[9]

Those who evangelize, then, are "working together" with God (II Cor. 6:1), and if they follow Paul's example they will never allow themselves to forget that all the power that comes through their witness, and all the fruit that results from it, is from God and not from themselves. I preached Christ crucified to you, wrote Paul to the Corinthians, in such a way that "your faith should not rest on the wisdom of men, but on the power of God.... I planted, Apollos watered, but God was causing the growth" (I Cor. 2:5; 3:6, cf. Acts 19:9f., where the "many people" in verse 10 are those Corinthians whom the Lord purposed to call to himself through Paul's preaching). Our gospel came to you, wrote Paul to the Thessalonians, "in power and in the Holy Spirit and with full conviction" (I Thess. 1:5); that explains why they received it "for what it really is, the word of God, which also performs its work in you who believe" (2:13). Paul sees their conviction as the fruit of their election, and so thanks God for their faith, which was his gift to them (1:2-5; 2:13). Luke shows the same perspective when he says of Lydia, "the Lord opened her heart to respond to the things spoken by Paul" (Acts 16:14).

Recognition that all the power and fruit of the word is from God and not from any human source does not, however, mean that the evangelist may disregard the human factors in persuasion. The ordinary principles of effective persuasion are not changed just because in a special way God is working through them. Paul was very conscious of the human factors in persuasion (cogency of statement, and empathetic concern), and he was most conscientious in observing them. He set no limit to what he would do to ensure that he did not, through personal insensitiveness or cultural inertia, set barriers and stumbling-blocks in the way of men's coming to Christ. "I have made myself a slave to all, that I might win the more. And to the Jews I became as a Jew, that I might win Jews ... to those who are without law, as without law ... that I might win those who are without law. To the weak I became weak, that I might win the weak; I have become all things to all men, that I may by all means save some" (I Cor. 9:19-22). It was to remove possible stumbling-blocks for Jews that Paul had Timothy circumcised (Acts 16:3) and also, it seems, Titus, though as he stressed he was under no compulsion to do this (Gal. 2:3). Paul's loving, imaginative adaptability in the service of truth and people is a shining example to all who engage in evangelism, and it cannot be pondered too often or taken too seriously.

But what in the last analysis determined Paul's view of his role as a "Christian persuader"[10] was his awareness that his ministry, like all Christian ministry, was both the form and the means of Christ's. It was Jesus Christ Himself, the risen Savior and enthroned Lord, who in and through Paul's evangelism "preached peace" (Eph. 2:17), and made his voice heard (Eph. 4:21; cf. John 10:16,27), and drew men to him (cf. John 12:32). The faith that sustained Paul in evangelism was that Christ would continue to do this, as in fact he had been doing everywhere that the gospel went (cf. Col. 1:6); and when Paul thought of his achievements in evangelism, his way of describing them was as *"what Christ has accomplished through me, resulting in the obedience of the Gentiles by word and deed ... in the power of the Spirit"* (Rom. 15:18f.). To say that Paul, and all others who evangelize, work for the Lord is not untrue, but to speak of them as working together with him is truer, and to speak of him as working through them is the most profound and precise truth of all.

There is one further way in which the concept of evangelism which we are building up needs extension, namely by reference to the message proclaimed. In the Bible, evangelism appears as *a work of God through men proclaiming Jesus Christ, and the new community in him.* Christian communication is not evangelism unless the full truth about Jesus is set forth. It is not enough to speak of the attractiveness of his person while omitting reference to the atoning significance of his work, as old-style liberals did. Nor is it enough to speak of his death as a sacrifice for sin if one declines to confess his deity, as Jehovah's Witnesses do. Nor will it suffice to dwell on his earthly life and impact while remaining agnostic about his physical resurrection, present reign, and approaching personal return, as is the common radical way. It is not adequate to point to Jesus' personal relationship with his disciples two millennia ago if we do not also declare that the glorified Jesus, though temporarily withdrawn from our sight, offers us just such a personal relationship today. For it is essentially this relationship that the Christian gospel is about. Jesus lives, and personal discipleship goes on. This, which from one standpoint is the central meaning of Jesus' resurrection and the outpouring of the Spirit, is from the same standpoint the evangelist's central message. And the new community belongs to this central message, for the call to become a disciple is also a call to become a partner with all other disciples. The question whether the church is part of the gospel used to be debated with some heat. If "church" is taken to mean a particular denomination or organization, viewed as an institute of salvation through its established channels of grace, the answer is certainly no. But if "church" means the brotherhood of God's children by adoption, into which all believers come and in the fellowship of which they find their God-intended fulness of life, then the answer must be yes. When John Wesley said that there is nothing so un-Christian as a solitary Christian, he spoke a profound truth. The gospel invites to fellowship, not merely with the Father and the Son, but with the saints too. What God calls us to is not "flight of the alone to the Alone," but life as a son in his worldwide family, where the rule is that our Father provides for each of us through the ministry of our brothers.

By the light of our concept of evangelism as a work of God we can now assess definitions of evangelism as a human activity. There is no reason why we should not define evangelism in this way, so long as subordination to God's purpose and dependence on God's power are duly stressed. Perhaps the best-known definition of this kind is that of the Archbishops' Committee on evangelism in the Church of England, which in 1918 stated that to evangelize is "so to present Christ Jesus in the power of the Holy Spirit, that men shall come to put their trust in God through Him, to accept Him as their Saviour, and serve Him as their King in the fellowship of His Church." In my book, *Evangelism and the Sovereignty of God*, I applauded this definition in all respects save its consecutive-clause wording, "that men *shall* come," which implies that the criterion of whether a particular activity is evangelism or not is whether or not it succeeds in converting anyone. The wording needed, I urged, was "that men *may* come," so that evangelism as an activity is unambiguously defined in terms of purpose rather than of consequence.[11] The resultant definition would then correspond exactly with the crisper formula of Michael Green: "Evangelism . . . is proclaiming the good news of salvation to men and women with a view to their conversion to Christ and incorporation in his church."[12] However, C. Peter Wagner takes me to task for making this proposal, in a rather muddled section of his otherwise stimulating book *Frontiers in Missionary Strategy*.[13] The thesis Wagner wants to establish is that it is insufficient to conceive of evangelism as "presence" if this does not lead on to proclamation, and that proclamation in turn is insufficient if it does not issue in attempts at persuasion. This is certainly right. The need for positive attempts to persuade was one of the points which my own book most labored (see pp. 48-53, 75-82, 85, 92f., 99f., 103-106, 119-121). It is, therefore, disconcerting to find Wagner (who, incidentally, quotes Green's definition with warm approval) calling me "one who has considered the options and come out on the side of proclamation evangelism"—i. e., a view of evangelism which sees proclamation, not as a *means*, but as an *alternative* to persuasion.[14] I can assure Wagner (and my book is evidence) that that is an option I *never* considered!

Wagner seems to be pleading for two things. One is, uninhibited though non-manipulative attempts to persuade unbelievers to turn to Christ. He wants to see a vigorous pressing of "the well-meant gospel offer," the "free offer" of Christ, the invitation to "whosoever will" to take the water of life, the call to that exercise of faith which is at once the sinner's need and his duty. With this, in principle, I hope everyone will agree; certainly, as an admirer of Richard Baxter, Joseph Alleine, George Whitefield, Jonathan Edwards and C. H. Spurgeon, I do. The second thing Wagner advocates is the use of a pragmatic, short-term calculus of "success" in church-planting and church-growth as a guide to where it is, and is not, right to deploy further missionary and evangelistic resources. This is much more disputable, but we cannot pursue discussion of it here.

Let me round off this section by quoting one further definition—Dr. George W. Peters' analysis of "evangelization" as "the authoritative presentation of the gospel of Jesus Christ as revealed in the Bible in relevant and intelligible terms, in a persuasive manner with the definite purpose of making Christian converts. It is a presentation-penetration-permeation-confrontation that not only elicits but demands a decision. It is preaching the gospel of Jesus Christ for a verdict.[15] Though there is no explicit reference here to the power and purpose of God or the church of Christ, the central emphasis on persuasion and conversion is in itself entirely right.

Educational Evangelism

One recurring problem when revivalist patterns of evangelism are followed, whether in single churches or in the "mass evangelism" of citywide campaigns, is that they allow so little room for instruction. From this it follows that where people are ignorant of biblical basics, these methods become inappropriate. Wisely did R. B. Kuiper say: "Historically the appeal of mass evangelism has been largely to the will and the emotions. That holds of the evangelistic preaching of both Wesley and Whitefield, to a limited extent to that of Jonathan Edwards, and most certainly to that of Dwight L. Moody, Charles G. Finney, Billy Sunday, and the Gypsy Smiths of more recent times. There was some justification for the nature of that appeal. All the aforenamed evangelists had good reason to assume on the part of their audiences a measure of knowledge of the basic teachings of Christianity. Today that assumption is no longer valid. . . . The general populace is well-nigh abysmally ignorant of Bible history and Bible doctrine, as well as Bible ethics. In consequence, evangelistic preaching must today be first of all instructive."[16] Paul spoke of "the gospel, for which I was appointed a preacher... *and a teacher*" (II Tim. 1:10f.), and said of Christ, "we proclaim him... *teaching every man* with all wisdom" (Col. 1:28). In both texts the reference to teaching is explanatory of the reference to preaching; Paul saw himself as a teaching preacher, an educational evangelist, and it is vitally important at the present time that we should confine ourselves to patterns of evangelistic practice which allow for thorough instruction, after Paul's example. For there is in fact a good deal to be conveyed.

If we ask, What is the evangelistic message?, the New Testament seems to show that there are essentially five points on which instruction must be given.

First, the gospel is a message about *God;* telling us that He is our maker, in whom we exist and move each moment and in whose hands, for good or ill, we always are, and that we, his creatures, were made to worship and serve Him and to live for His glory. These are the foundation-truths of theism, and upon them the gospel is built. The Jews of New Testament days, with Old Testament faith behind them, knew these things, and when the apostles preached to Jews they could take them for granted. But when Paul preached to Gentiles, whose background was polytheistic, it was with theism that he had to start. So, when the Athenians asked him to explain his talk about Jesus and the resurrection, he began by telling them about God, the creator. "God... made the world... he himself gives to all life and breath and all things... and he made... every nation... that they should seek God" (Acts 17:24-27). This was not, as is sometimes supposed, a piece of philosophical apologetic which Paul afterwards regretted, but the first and basic lesson in theistic faith. Modern men are for the most part as ignorant about creation and creaturehood as were the ancient Athenians; like Paul, therefore, we must start in evangelizing them by telling them of the Creator whom they have forgotten to remember, and go on from there.

Second, the gospel is a message about *sin.* It defines sin as failure to meet the holy Creator's total claim, and it diagnoses sin in us, telling us that we are helpless slaves of our own rebelliousness, showing ourselves under the righteous judgment of God, and assuring us that nothing we do for ourselves can put us right. Not till we have begun to grasp these things can we see what it means to say that Jesus Christ saves from sin. All sorts of awarenesses of need are symptoms of sin; much of the task of evangelistic instruction is to take occasion from these symptoms to diagnose the real disease, and thus bring to light "the problem behind the problem," our fundamental wrongness with God.

Third, the gospel is a message about *the person and work of Christ;* an interpreted story of the earthly life, death, resurrection and reign of God's Son. Both the facts and the meaning must be given. Whether or not we use the technical terms, "incarnation," "atonement" and so forth, we must teach what they express—who Jesus was, in relation both to the Father and to us, and what He did as His Father's will for us. It is sometimes said that it is the presentation of Christ's person, rather than of doctrines about Him, that draws sinners to His feet, and it is certainly true that it is the living Christ who saves, and that a theory of atonement, however orthodox, is no substitute for a savior. But Jesus of Nazareth cannot be known as the living Christ if we are unaware that He was eternal God and that His passion, His judicial murder, was really His redeeming action of bearing away men's sins. We cannot see Jesus as a personal savior till we see this, nor can we know how to approach Him till we have learned that the man of Galilee now reigns as God's king, and must be hailed as such.

Fourth, the Gospel is a message about *new birth*, telling us that our plight in sin is so great that nothing less than a supernatural renewing of us can save us. There has to be a wholly new beginning, through the power of the Holy Spirit.

Fifth, the gospel summons us to *faith, repentance and discipleship*. Faith is not a mere feeling of confidence, nor repentance and discipleship. Faith is not a mere feeling of confidence, nor repentance a mere feeling of remorse; both are dynamic states of the whole man. Faith is credence and conviction regarding the gospel message, and it is more; born of self-despair, it is essentially a casting and resting of oneself on the promises of Christ and the Christ of those promises. Repentance is a changed attitude of heart and mind, leading to a new life of denying self and serving the Saviour as king in self's place. And discipleship is a matter of relating oneself to the living, exalted Christ as a learner and a follower, and to the rest of Christ's disciples as one who longs both to learn from them and to give to them, and who knows that his master's will is for him to be in their company.

This, in outline, is the evangelistic message, and it needs to be thoroughly taught everywhere where it is not already thoroughly known. It is the Holy Spirit's work to make sinners repent and believe, but it is our task and responsibility to make sure that they are clear what the gospel is, how it affects them, and why and how they should respond to it; and until we are sure that a person has grasped these things, we are hardly in a position to press him to commit himself to Christ, for it is not yet clear that he is in a position really and responsibly to do so. Whatever means and structures we use in evangelism, all the points listed must be taught. If we tried to short-circuit the process of instruction and to precipitate "decisions" without it, we should merely produce psychological upsets; people would come to our vestries and counselling sessions in an agitated state; they would go through motions of commitment at our bidding, but when the shock wore off it would appear that their decision meant nothing save that now they are to a greater or less extent "gospel-hardened." And if a few proved to be truly converted, that would be despite our methods rather than because of them.

It is no part of my present task to attempt judgments on any particular ways of evangelism that are practiced today, but it is surely plain from what has been said that there can be no safer or more natural milieu for evangelism than the steady teaching, witnessing and nurturing of the local church.

Response to the Gospel

This essay is seeking to spell out a normative theological concept of evangelism, by which any attempted reformation of evangelism in our day will need to be controlled. One further matter requires discussion for the clarifying of this concept, namely the nature of the response which evangelism requires. So far, we have spoken of it as conversion, involving faith, repentance and discipleship; but this formula is not clear enough in its meaning, and we must take the analysis further.

The common pietistic and revivalist understanding, present at presuppositional level even when it is not made theologically explicit, is that the gospel of God is meant to induce a characteristic *conversion-experience*. This is conceived as a compound of two elements: the experience of receiving, and committing oneself to, the God and the Christ of the gospel, and the experience of receiving assurance from that God, so that one knows oneself pardoned and accepted by him. The relative emphasis on these two elements has varied: in the eighteenth century, for example, the stress was on assurance ("finding peace"), in the twentieth it has been on commitment ("decision for Christ"); but it is constantly assumed that where there is one there will also be the other. In the pietistic-revivalist tradition, evangelistic procedures (meetings, sermons, tracts, conversational techniques) have all been shaped by the desire that God should use them to induce conversion-experiences, and the belief that this is precisely what He wills to do. But here some comments must be made.

First, it must be said that while a conversion-experience, like any other particular conscious encounter with a gracious God, is a precious gift, and while no adult can turn to God and live to God without some experiences of this encounter (the Holy Spirit will see to that), the Bible teaches no doctrine of God-given experiences as such. It defines God's purpose and work in men's lives in terms, not of experiences, but of relationships, and though relationships issue in experiences, the two things are not the same. God's work in our lives, whereby He creates and deepens our love-relationships with Himself, is more than experience (for it is an actual transformation of our being, in ways which do not yet fully appear), and it is beyond experience (for the experiences which are its product are far less than its measure; much of what God does in us is not directly experienced). To say, then, what is true—that God wills through our evangelism to work in unbelievers and call them effectually to himself—is something bigger than, and somewhat different from, saying that God will through our evangelism induce conversion-experiences.

Third, it must be said that what the Bible looks for in Christians is not the consciousness of a conversion-experience, but the evidence of a converted state; and its angle of interest when dealing with actual conversions is motivational rather than psychological—that is, its purpose is not to tell us what men who turned to God felt like, so that we can imaginatively put ourselves in their shoes, but to show us how God actually met them and moved them to go his way. The signs of convertedness are simply the marks of discipleship, the marks, that is, of being one of the Lord's *learners* —namely, a structured knowledge of God in Christ, which the learner seeks constantly to deepen and augment; a practical recognition of total and controlling commitment to God and His will, and to Christ and His people; and an awareness that knowing and enjoying God is man's true life (just as it is his chief end), which leads him to press on resolutely to know his Lord better, at any cost and by any road, and to look ahead with eagerness to the glory that is promised when Jesus comes again.

Fourth, it must be said that the more we concentrate on inducing, isolating and identifying conversion-experiences, the more risk we run of misunderstanding and misrepresenting the course of actual experience. For it is not always possible to isolate the moment of conversion. God leads some into a firm faith-relationship with himself by a series of imperceptible steps, so that the precise moment of passage from death to life cannot be picked out for inspection. (This is the case in many Bible biographies.) Conversely, it is only too possible to induce in the susceptible experiences of supposed conversion which do not develop into discipleship or a meaningful church commitment, but issue in nothing—as happened in the Cornish revivals of the last century, in which folk "got converted" time and again without any real change of heart; and as seems to have happened during the first decade of Evangelism in Depth in Latin America.[17]

What this means is that in all evangelism our aim must be nothing less than to make men Christ's disciples in the community of disciples; that we must constantly check our evangelistic structures to ensure that this aim comes through clearly; and that we leave people in no doubt that the response we hope to see in them is convertedness rather than a particular conversion-experience. Also, the question arises whether, instead of isolating individuals in order to pursue with them the issues of personal commitment, which is a basic revivalist technique, we should not give priority to evangelizing them in their natural human groupings—in the West, for instance, the nuclear family; in other countries, the extended family (the clan), or the tribe—seeking a discipleship-commitment from the group, and from individuals as members of it. This would be a step back towards the evangelistic style of the apostolic age, which, as Harry R. Boer notes, was marked by "the conversion of *families* or *households*. The Church was not built up of so many individual Christians but of *basic social units,*, of *organic wholes*, and these units, these wholes, were the fundamental cells of society, namely *families.*[18] Is this part of what the reformation of evangelism in our day might mean?

The view of evangelism put forward in this essay is conceived in terms of God and His message primarily, and of man and his methods only secondarily. It affirms that what man says and does in evangelism must be determined by what God is doing, and that the divine message itself must determine the aims and methods of the human messengers. To discuss in detail how this approach might bear on contemporary evangelistic practice is beyond my scope—and, I think, my competence. I limit myself to offering an overall concept of evangelism, crystallized from Scripture as best I can; and I hope it may make some small contribution towards the reform and renewal of evangelism which, on any showing, is a major need at this time.

FOOTNOTES

[1] Michael Green, *Evangelism in the Early Church* (London: Hodder and Stoughton, 1970), p. 7.

[2] The quotations are from *The Death of Christ* (London: Hodder and Stoughton, 1902), p. vii; *The Expositor* (June 1901), p. 440; and James Moffatt's "Introduction" to *Letters of Principal James Denney to his Family and Friends* (London: Hodder and Stoughton, 1921), pp. xii f.; all cited by John Randolph Taylor, *God Loves Like That! The Theology of James Denney* (London: SCM Press, 1962), pp. 29f.

[3] B. B. Warfield comments on Finney's Pelagian doctrine of plenary ability in *Perfectionism* (New York: Oxford University Press, 1931), II, pp. 173 ff.

[4] On Moody, cf. W. G. McLoughlin, *Modern Revivalism: Charles Grandison Finney to Billy Graham* (New York: The Ronald Press Company, 1959).

[5] Cf., for evidence of this, *Eye of the Storm: The Great Debate in Mission*, ed. Donald McGavran (Waco: Word Books, 1972), and *The Evangelical Response to Bangkok*, ed. Ralph D. Winter (South Pasadena: William Carey Library, 1973).

[6] J. G. Davies, *Dialogue with the World* (London: SCM Press, 1967), p. 15.

[7] C. Peter Wagner, *Frontiers in Missionary Strategy* (Chicago: Moody Press, 1971), p. 126.

[8] R. B. Kuiper, *God-centered Evangelism: a Presentation of the Scriptural Theology of Evangelism* (Grand Rapids: Baker Book House, 1963), p. 95.

[9] J. I. Packer, *Evangelism and the Sovereignty of God* (London: Inter-Varsity Fellowship, 1961), p. 85.

[10] Title of a perceptive book by Leighton Ford on the work of a professional evangelist (New York: Harper and Row, 1966).

[11] Packer, *op. cit.*, pp. 37 ff.

[12] Green, *op. cit.*, p. 7. My definition tallies also with that of the World Congress on Evangelism in Berlin, which is an expansion of that given by the Archbishops' Committee: "Evangelism is the proclamation of the Gospel of the crucified and risen Christ, the only Redeemer of men, according to the Scriptures, with the purpose of persuading condemned and lost sinners to put their trust in God by receiving and accepting Christ as Savior through the power of the Holy Spirit, and to serve Christ as Lord in every calling in life and in the fellowship of his church, looking towards the day of his coming in glory" (quoted from Wagner, *op. cit.*, p. 133).

[13] *Ibid.*, pp. 124-134.

[14]"Proclamation evangelism," Wagner explains, "measures success against the yardstick of how many people hear and understand the gospel message. This is often reported in terms of how many people are reached by attending a certain evangelistic campaign listening to a certain radio broadcast, or reading a certain piece of evangelistic literature" (*ibid.*, p. 132ff.).

[15]George W. Peters, *A Biblical Theology of Missions* (Chicago: Moody Press, 1972), p. 11.

[16]Kuiper, *op. cit.*, p. 163.

[17]Cf. Wagner, *op. cit.*, pp. 139-160.

[18]Harry R. Boer, *Pentecost and Missions* (London: Lutterworth Press, 1961), p. 165.

2.
METHODS AND STRATEGY IN THE EVANGELISM OF THE EARLY CHURCH

MICHAEL GREEN

When a movement grows from a dozen peasants in an unimportant corner of the world, to be the official religion of the civilized world inside 300 years; when it is sufficiently independent of that civilization to survive its fall, and indeed the fall of every successive civilization since; when it is universal enough in its appeal to win millions of converts in all sectors of the globe, among all types of men, belonging to every race, culture, and personality type—then it is arguable that such a movement has got something. It is also arguable that we have a good deal to learn from its strategy and tactics, its methods and approaches.

That movement is Christianity. The church of today is heir to the revolutionary forces which changed the face of the world in the decades folowing the death and resurrection of Jesus. And yet, one would never guess it. The idea of the modern church being a revolutionary, invading force is laughable in the West though readily understandable in Indonesia, Korea, Latin America, and many parts of Africa. Certainly a Western Christian such as myself can only hang his head in shame when comparing our own approach to evangelism with that of the early Christians, and with that of contemporary Christians in many developing countries. Let us just set out some of the more obvious contrasts.

The early church made evangelism their number one priority. Today it comes far down the list. It is widely agreed that one of the best reports ever prepared and presented in the Church of England was that entitled, *Towards the Conversion of England*, thirty years ago. It was masterly, but the trouble is that it has never been implemented. The matter is not deemed sufficiently important. The same can be said of most plans formulated in many denominations in many nations.

The early church had a deep compassion for men without Christ. Many sections of the modern church are far more convinced that it much matters whether you have Christ or not. Other religions are nearly, if not quite, as good a way to God; humanists live blameless lives; and in any case, it will all come right in the end—God is far too nice to damn anyone.

The early church was very flexible in its preaching of the Good News, but utterly opposed to syncretism (mixing other elements with the Gospel) of any sort. Many parts of the modern church tend to be rigid in their evangelistic categories, but are inclined to play a great deal with syncretism, as Lesslie Newbigin has forcefully pointed out in *The Finality of Christ.*

The early church was very open to the leading of the Holy Spirit; in every evangelistic advance recorded in Acts it is the Spirit who is the motivator and energizer. In the modern church of the West, managerial skills, committee meetings, and endless discussion are thought essential for evangelism; prayer and dependence on the Spirit seem often to be optional extras.

The early church was not unduly minister-conscious. There is notorious difficulty in attempting to read back any modern ministerial pattern into the New Testament records. Today, everything tends to center around the minister. The paid servant of the church is expected to engage in God-talk, but not others.

In the early church, every man was expected to be a witness to Christ. Today witness is at a discount compared with dialogue; and it is only expected of certain gifted clergy at best, not of run-of-the-mill Christians.

In the early church, buildings were unimportant; they did not have any during the period of their greatest advance. Today they seem all-important to many Christians; their upkeep consumes the money and interest of the members, often plunges them into debt, and isolates them from those who do not go to church. Indeed, even the word has changed meaning. "Church" no longer means a company of people, as it did in New Testament times. These days it means a building.

In the early church, evangelism was a natural, spontaneous "chattering" of good news. It was engaged in continuously by all types of Christians as a matter of course and of privilege. Today, it is spasmodic, heavily organized, and usually dependent on the skills and enthusiasm of the visiting specialist.

In the early church, the policy was to go out to where people were, and make disciples of them. Today it is to invite people along to churches, where they do not feel at home, and get them to hear the preaching of the Gospel. Today's church attempts suction, invitation, "in-drag"; the early church practiced explosion, invasion, outreach.

In the early church, whole communities seem to have been converted at once. In the atomized church of the West, individualism has run riot, and evangelism, like much else, tends to come to its climax in a one-to-one encounter.

In the early church the maximum impact was made by the changed lives and quality of community among the Christians. Today, much Christian life-style is almost indistinguishable from that of non-Christians, and much church fellowship is conspicuous for its coolness.

These are just some of the contrasts between the church of yesterday and the church of today in the matter of evangelism—contrasts which encourage us to examine afresh the message of the early Christians and the methods they adopted.

1. The message

I shall not expand too much on the pattern of the New Testament proclamation, because so much work has been done on it in recent years, since the publication of C. H. Dodd's *The Apostolic Preaching and its Development*. Throughout the Gospel of Mark, Hebrews, the Pauline Letters, I Peter, and Acts, it is possible to discern the main bones of much early Christian preaching. The age of fulfillment has dawned. God has at last sent his Messiah, Jesus. He died in shame upon a Cross. He rose again from the tomb and is even now Lord, seated at the Father's right hand. The proof of his vindication lies in the gift of the Holy Spirit. And he will come again to judge the world at the conclusion of human history. Therefore, repent, believe, and be baptized into Christ and joined to the church. Such would be a rough summary of a pattern of proclamation which can be found, explicit or implicit, in a broad variety of strands within the New Testament. This was the Good News that they told men (our "evangelism" comes from the Greek word "martyr" which meant "witness" before it came to denote the witness who sealed his testimony with his blood). They varied a great deal in the stress they laid on different elements in the story. But they were all convinced that in Jesus, God's final act of deliverance, the climax of all his saving and revealing activity throughout Israel's history had begun. In particular, it was the death and resurrection (never the one without the other) of Jesus that formed the focus of their message. This Jesus, who had tasted death for every man, and himself had taken responsibility for human wrongdoing, was alive—indeed he was enthroned in the universe. As such, he offered both pardon and power to those who committed themselves to him. The long-awaited Spirit of God was his gift to believers.

Thus God's law was no longer something exterior to man, threatening him. The longings of Jeremiah and Ezekiel were fulfilled in the inauguration of this New Covenant, wherein the Spirit of God became resident within the very hearts of his people, as the pledge of their acceptance, the helper in their prayers, the compass in their morals, the power for godly living, and the first installment of heaven.

This is the general gist of the message preached by those early evangelists. It was not an easy one for Jews to accept—no circumcision, no Torah, no sabbath, a crucified Messiah (contradiction in terms!), a church which included Gentiles, and was entered by baptism: All this was anathema to the Jew. It was no easier for the Greek world to accept—for it was Eastern, exclusive, new, of doubtful morality, politically suspect, socially disruptive, and intellectually ridiculous. Yet this was the message which the Christians continued to preach. When addressing Gentile believers they added three introductory themes: you can see them in the Acts sermons at Lystra and Athens, to backward and to intellectual alike. They were, first, an exposition of the one true God; second, an exposure of idolatry; and third, the story of Jesus, through whom alone this invisible God can be made known to us without any shred of idolatry.

There are three aspects of their message to which we might profitably pay attention.

a. It was Christ-centered. Jesus was the center of what they proclaimed. It might be Paul at Athens proclaiming, "Jesus and resurrection," or Philip in the desert, "telling him the Good News of Jesus," but always Christ was the kernel of their message. God had made Jesus both Messiah (Christ) and Lord (a name used both for heathen gods, and for Yahweh in the Old Testament). So central was "Christ" (Messiah—God's ultimate deliverer) to their interpretation of who Jesus was, that they earned themselves a nickname—*Christians*. Is this centrality of Jesus not something that the contemporary evangelist could well ponder? He might be interpreted as Son of Man, the High Priest according to the Melchizedek order, the Suffering Servant, the Prophet like Moses, or the author, sustainer, and goal of the whole universe (as in Colossians I and Ephesians I). No matter. It was to Jesus they returned, Jesus whom they announced. Incidentally it is interesting to notice, in view of the current radical divide between the Jesus of history and the Christ of faith, and the supposed irrelevance of the story of Jesus to the proclamation of the Gospel of the living Christ, that the early Christians would have none of it. They wrote and used the Gospel stories, the parables and miracles, to preach the historical Jesus as the Lord, the Christ, whom they worshiped.

b. It was flexible. This is where Dodd's book falls short: he does not sufficiently allow for the flexibility in preaching the Gospel which marked those early Christians. When studying the approaches of Christians to Jews and Gentiles, rich and poor, clever and unintelligent, over the first two centuries I was amazed at the variety in their proclamation. The Gospel was born, of course, in a Palestinian milieu. Old Testament models came readily enough to hand. Jesus was seen as the fulfillment of Daniel's Son of Man, Isaiah's Suffering Servant, the anointed prophet, priest, and king of various Old Testament strands: he was the exalted Lord of Psa. 110:1, the prophet like Moses, and the ultimate successor to David.

But on Gentile soil it was different. The first evangelists engaged in extensive retranslation work, not so much of words, as of concepts. They did not begin by quoting Old Testament texts; they started from the felt needs of the hearers, and used imagery that would communicate with them. Thus we find Paul at Athens proceeding inductively from what he sees around him; the altar to an unknown God. In Romans we find him speaking of adoption, a concept as familiar among the pagans as it was alien to Hebrew culture. In I Cor. 15:3-5 we find the core of the primitive preaching to the Jews: Jesus died for our sins, and was raised the third day. Given the background of the profoundly ethical God of the Old Testament, "How shall a man be right with God?" was the critical question for any thoughtful Jew. Paul shows how it is answered in Christ crucified and risen. But he gives a very different interpretation of that Cross and resurrection to the Gentiles in Col. 2:15, I Tim. 3:16. Here it is not so much sin which oppresses (conviction of sin is rarely found outside a monotheistic culture) but bondage; bondage to the various demonic powers which hold men in control, particularly Fate *(heimarmene)* and Necessity *(ananche)*. To men with such a problem, the incarnation of Jesus and his triumphant resurrection were the key points to stress. Indeed, a whole theological emphasis depicting Christ as conqueror springs from looking at the resurrection in this light. And it certainly brought deliverance to pagan men, obsessed as they were with the sense of the demonic. "We are above Fate," cries Tatian, "and instead of the demons which deceive we have learned one Master who does not deceive." The very word, "Lord," so often attached to Jesus in the Pauline letters, is meant to distinguish him sharply from the "many lords" mentioned in I Cor. 8:5, who had held his readers in thralldom. Similarly, the accent shifts from the Kingdom of God, which Jesus himself heralded so consistently, to "eternal life" or "salvation," words which conveyed the sense of Jesus' message more clearly to Gentile hearers. To a world which, under Stoic influence, conceived of a universal Reason (Logos) underlying the universe, a Reason in which all men naturally had part, Jesus is proclaimed in John I (and similarly in Col. 1:15ff; Heb. 1:1ff) as *the* universal Reason underlying all there is; this Reason was God himself, active since the creation of the world. But all men do not naturally partake of the eternal Logos; they are rebels, and only those who receive him have the right to call themselves sons of God. And thus the idea, common in Stoic circles, is made the vehicle of Christian preaching.

There were other men in antiquity who would have latched on immediately to this Logos idea; men of the neo-Platonist school, who conceived of it as the eternal order of pure reality, somehow copied, however inadequately, in all things that are good and true in this world of space and time. "Well," says St. John, "if that is how you think, let me tell you something: there is one single area in the universe where the ideal has become real, where the archetype has broken through, where the Word has become flesh. And that is in the life, death, and resurrection of Jesus Christ." John 1:14 is in fact, a powerful philosophical claim for the absoluteness of Jesus of Nazareth.

Clearly, there was nothing inflexible about these early Christians in the New Testament period. Nor was there in the succeeding century or two, as the Gospel spread. You find philosophers like Justin and Tatian retaining their philosopher's robe and arguing the truth of the Christian philosophy against all comers. You find them looking not only to the Old Testament but to the myths of Homer and Hesiod for truths that would help to illuminate the person and work of Jesus. They were convinced that all truth is God's truth. Therefore they rejoiced when they found that some of the ancient heathen poets or philosophers had spoken true things which were endorsed in the Gospel of Christ.

I used to think it was odd (if not worse!) of Clement of Rome in the nineties of the first century, to use the mythical bird, the phoenix, before I had seen the picture of the phoenix at Pompeii (a city destroyed in A.D. 79) and read what the painter, hungering for immortality, had written below it. "O phoenix, you are a lucky thing!" Then I realized how wise an apologist Clement had been in relating the resurrection of the Lord to the very symbol of need which the painter of the phoenix had revealed. Like Paul, Clement had become all things to all men, so that by all means he might save some.

Of course, the early Christians made two types of mistakes in this attempt to preach the Gospel meaningfully into their situation. Gnosticism which was a way of salvation through knowledge, was the fruit of uncritically accepting pagan frames of reference, just as syncretism is today. And Ebionism, which stressed the humanity of Jesus to the exclusion of his deity, was the fruit of rigid determination to preach Jesus as "Son of God" to Jews who could not possibly hear those words without the feeling that it was blasphemy (though other christological formulations, just as absolute, could have been acceptable to them). These two Christian heresies of the second century were the direct result in the one case of uncritical cross-cultural relativism, and in the other of soldiering obstinately on using the language of Zion and expecting people to understand it if they were not gospel hardened. The implications for today are obvious. *Honest to God*, by Bishop John Robinson, was a genuine attempt to communicate the Christian faith to men who were alienated by the way most clergy preached it: the fantastic sales of the book show what a vast number of people were touched by such an approach; unfortunately, it was no longer the Gospel of Jesus Christ that was communicated. (Robinson attempts to communicate the Gospel to the so-called "modern man come of age" by removing what are believed to be unpalatable supernatural elements.) Surely we are called back to that daring flexibility of the early Chistians, letting the world set the agenda, and answering it imaginatively in the light of the New Testament witness to Jesus. If we take the variety of the New Testament itself as our model, we shall never be monochrome or dull: if we submit our retranslated message to the judgment of the New Testament we shall not erode the Gospel in the process of translating it. This is a perilously knife-edge operation, but every evangelist must undertake it if he is to be faithful both to Christ and to his own generation.

c. *It was definite.* Cristianity took root in unwelcoming pagan soil. The old pantheon of gods was receiving constant additions as the Roman Empire expanded, and new deities were absorbed. It would have been easy enough to get Jesus accepted on these terms. Alternatively, there were the mystery religions; remarkably Christian in a way, with their stress on a dying and rising god—the year deity, the fertility god. Jesus could have been identified with such a deity. Alternatively, there was the imperial cult: Caesar was Lord, and if only Christians had been willing to accord him divine honors, they would not have been persecuted for the loyalty they gave to Jesus. Again, there were the philosophical schools, coming together a good deal by the first century, and having a more religious flavor about them, as Platonic idealism, mixed with high Stoic ethics, sought not only the Absolute but God.

Now it is interesting that the Christians used all these paths in order to bring men to Christ, but they did not surrender to any of them. Paul was willing to be misunderstood as adding two new deities to the pantheon when preaching "Jesus and Ressurection" at Athens, so long as he had the opportunity to explain to the assembled multitude that he was doing no such thing! In that same address he used concepts familiar to both the Epicureans and the Stoics, and yet he was unfashionable enough to tell them both that the one thing they needed to do was to repent! And when Christians said, "Jesus is Lord," though it sounded rather like the imperial acclamations, in fact it was assigning exclusive divine honors to Jesus.

So while the early Christians would use any pathway to Christ, it was to Christ that these pathways unambiguously led. There was no hint of compromise, of syncretism. Paul addressed the Colossians when a syncretizing heresy was under way. *"Jesus and . . . a variety of mediators"* was their cry. Paul used much of their language. But he claimed an utterly exclusive position for his Lord. Whatever other "principalities and powers" there might be, Jesus was their creator and their Lord. He was the origin, the goal, and the principle of coherence in the whole universe, and his death on the Cross the only way of access to God. Did the false teachers speak of *pleroma*, the supposed habitat of these intermediating powers? Fine, says Paul, so long as you are clear about one thing. "In Christ lives all the fullness *(pleroma)* of the Godhead in bodily form." Great flexibility in presentation, then, but great firmness on content was his emphasis. And the content was Jesus, Creator, Savior, and Lord. To be sure they realized that other faiths contain much that is true. It would be strange if they did not. But they do not contain any truth about God that is not to be found in the Judaeo-Christian revelation, and they certainly contain a great deal of error. What is more, they do not provide any means of access to God whatsoever. That is provided uniquely by the One who came from God to reveal and to save.

The point is that no *man* can bridge the divide between the Holy and the sinful, between the Infinite and the finite, between God and man. The early Christians were convinced that God had visited his people in person, and accordingly were prepared to be martyred for their assertion that "there is salvation in no other; for there is no other name under heaven given to men whereby we must be saved" (Acts 4:12). Despite the flexibility of their message, it was always Christ-centered and always carried the implication of decision in repentance, faith, and baptism. Whether we look at the appeals to commitment in Acts, or turn to *2 Clement* (an early church document about A.D. 150) or the *Protrepticus* (an address to the Greeks by Clement of Alexandria, who wrote towards the end of the second century, seeking to win them over to Christianity), or to Gregory's fascinating account of the way in which that wise fisher of men and massive intellectual, Origen, hunted him out, taught him, intrigued him, and eventually brought him to Christ, the picture is uniform. The apostolic kerygma demanded a response. This was not something shallow or emotional, but touched the conscience, illuminated the understanding, brought the will into submission, and transformed the subsequent life. It was nothing less than a new birth.

2. The methods

There does not seem to have been anything very remarkable in the strategy and tactics of the early Christian mission. Indeed, it is doubtful if they had one. I do not believe they set out with any blueprint. They had an unquenchable conviction that Jesus was the key to life and death, happiness and purpose, and they simply could not keep quiet about him. The Spirit of Jesus within them drove them into mission. The tandem relationship between the Spirit bearing witness to Jesus and the believers bearing that witness (John 15:26f, Acts 1:7,8) was well understood among them, and the initiatives in evangelism which we read of in Acts are consistently laid at the door of the Lord the Spirit himself: effective mission does not spring from human blueprints. No, the nearest to a strategy those early Christians had was, perhaps, as follows:

a. They worked from the center outwards. "Beginning from Jerusalem" was the key word in Jesus' farewell charge to his disciples. And beginning from where they were, those twelve men swiftly grew by means of prayer, fellowship, a deep experience of the Spirit, and fearless preaching even in the face of persecution, into a body to whom God was adding fresh converts daily, and who filled the whole of Jerusalem with their teaching. Acts then traces, briefly, the spread of the Gospel into Judaea, then to Samaria, and from there to the uttermost parts of the earth. But always the policy seems to be to get the heart of the group hot, for only then will it be ready for fresh additions. The policy of so much modern evangelism is to drag people from the outside inwards; their policy was the opposite—to move from the inside outwards, and to evangelize, not on their own ground, but on other people's.

b. They were involved, yet mobile. They were indeed involved, totally involved. It is fascinating to find that in the early centuries of the church there was no division between those who told the good news and those who only listened to it. All were involved in the mission. You see this graphically portrayed in the spontaneous evangelistic sortie of nameless amateur evangelists from Jerusalem when Stephen had been killed and the remaining leaders were caught up in the city. The believers scattered, and "those that were scattered abroad went everywhere preaching the message." Celsus, in the second century, complains of the Christians at work, in the laundry, in the schoolroom, at the street corner, who were always jabbering away about their Jesus. Could any leading critic of Christianity today make the same charge?

Indeed, if one were to put it in a single sentence, the Early Church succeeded because every man was a missionary; the modern church fails because "missionary" has become a dirty word. These early Christians were all involved in the mission; and they were deeply involved in their communities as well. We read of doctors, teachers, agriculturalists, and others in normal jobs really caring for the communities in which they worked. Several times we have moving accounts of the way in which Christians tended victims in a plague at the risk of their own lives; and the love and self-sacrifice of Christians for their townsfolk even in the face of fierce opposition and martyrdom, won grudging praise from the pagans.

But with this sense of commitment to the local community, and involvement with its life, went a remarkable mobility. You got bishops like Irenaeus moving all around the known world. You got top intellectuals like Pantaenus leaving the Christian University of Alexandria of which he was the head, and going off to spread the Gospel among the "Indians." You got farmers moving from village to village to win fresh converts to their Lord. And you only need to glance back to the Acts, and look at Philip, Peter, Paul, or Aquila and Priscilla, to see how readily these early Christians were prepared to abandon home comforts for the sake of the Good News.

The question arises, are we? It would seem to me that the church today throughout the West at any rate, is paralyzed by a crippling lack of mobility. Granted that patterns of community, education and employment are so different, is there not, I wonder, a growing materialism that saps our total dedication to Christ and willingness to go anywhere and do anything for him if the Spirit should so lead?

c. They used their influence. It seems to me that many of these men planned their time with some care, conscious that they had but one life, and that they were determined to use it to the full for God. So they entered spheres where their influence would be felt to the maximum. That, presumably, helped to dictate the direction of the Pauline Missionary Journeys. Antioch was the third city in the empire; Philippi was a Roman colony and administrative capital; Thessalonica was the administrative center of Macedonia; Athens was the cultural center of the world; Corinth was the capital of the province of Achaea; Ephesus, where he spent three years, was the largest city in Asia; and Rome, his goal in the west, was mistress of the world.

It is hard to escape the conclusion that Paul, for one, was determined to use his talents to the full in the places where they would do the most good. Of course, such planning can degenerate into worldly ambition, but it need not, if the guidance of the Spirit is sought. Perhaps we should look for more of it today?

d. They exercised oversight. This is one of the intriguing factors in ancient evangelism which is not always looked after so well today. They were out from the start to consolidate gains. New disciples needed to be strengthened. Converts needed to be added to the church as well as to the Lord. They continued in the fellowship of the apostles, in their teaching, in their worship, and in their evangelism. There was, at least in some circles, some communalism of goods and life-style which may have been economic madness but bore eloquent testimony to the oneness in Christ which they talked about. That unity was maintained even as the church grew. The ancient splits between Jew and Samaritan, between Jew and Gentile, between bond and free, between male and female were not allowed to spoil the unity given by the Spirit. To this end, the apostles revisited their converts, they set up presbyters to look after them, they wrote letters to them, they sent messengers to them, and they prayed for them. Their unity so impressed the pagans of antiquity that they gradually began to call Christians "The Third Race"—not pagans, not Jews, but something radically different. From the most diverse backgrounds they had come together to form one new humanity in Christ. And wise diligent Christian oversight had been largely instrumental in maintaining this God-given unity.

e. They produced witnesses. This has already been touched on. It was the normal thing, not the pleasurable exception, for a Christian to become so thrilled with Christ that he had to find ways of expressing it to his non-Christian neighbors. Indeed, in contrast to much of our own effort these days, the early evangelists seem to have set themselves to increase the numbers of witnesses to Christ, not the number of those they could persuade to listen to addresses about Christ. They were out not to gather hearers, but to equip missionaries. This may not have been very self-conscious on their part, but it was a strategic decision of the utmost importance, and one which the modern church has scarcely begun to appreciate, unlike some of the sects, such as the Jehovah's Witnesses.

If these five factors seem to have been influential in determining the overall strategy of the early Christians, we may conclude by pointing out some of their tactical approaches which might prove suggestive for us today.

Their methods on the whole, while varied, were unremarkable. There is no key to instant success to be found by ransacking the methods used by the early church. Like us, they spoke in church. Like us, they spoke in the open air, though more frequently and with more directness, humor, and comeback from the audience than is common in the West. I believe that the rise and strength of the Pentecostals in South America is due, partly at least, to their insistence that members should bear witness to Christ upon the streets. After all, that is how it all began; and I am not persuaded that the day of the open air is over.

Like us, they visited. Ananias' visit to Saul of Tarsus is perhaps the classic case in the Acts. This again is a method that has fallen on evil days, and ministers persuade themselves that in this busy television-addicted age, it cannot be done, by themselves or laymen. It can be done and it must. I have led people to Christ simply by visiting them in their homes without any exposure to preaching, and many of you have done the same. It is an important method of evangelism.

Like us, they made use of literary evangelism. The written word was not so easy and cheap to produce in the days of handwritten books, but they did use this method; what, after all, are the Gospels intended for? But in particular they employed the Old Testament Scriptures. Just as Philip used verses in Isaiah 53 to open the eyes of the Ethiopian eunuch, so countless missionaries of the next two centuries followed suit. Men like Justin, Tatian, Pantaenus, and Athenagoras in the second century were won to the faith through reading the Scriptures of the Old Testament. We would be foolish to underestimate the converting power of the Word of God even in the absence of any human interpreter.

But if you asked me to name a few of the main methods used in evangelism then which are not given sufficient weight now, I should want to isolate four:

(i) The impact of *fellowship*. Whether you look at Jerusualem or Antioch; whether you read between the lines of the Epistles to the Philippians or Thessalonians; whether you pin your attention on Ephesus in the days of Paul and John, or Carthage in the days of Tertullian, the decisive importance of Christian fellowship is plain to see. These Christians embraced all the colors, all the classes, and all the untouchables of ancient society into one. They gave the impression of perpetual celebration, even in the face of death. Their services for worship gave rein for various spiritually gifted people to use their gift for the good of the whole. Their caring for each other in need became proverbial in antiquity. When people saw how these Christians loved one another; when they saw that in this society of Jesus the powers of the age to come were really exercised (prophecy, tongues, healing, alongside teaching, administration, and works of mercy), then they listened to the message of Jesus, who alone accounted for such a remarkable situation. Protestants for far too long have failed to recognize what the Catholics have appropriated, that the church is in a very real sense part of the Gospel. Unless the fellowship in the Christian assembly is far superior to that which can be found anywhere else in society, then the Christians can talk about the transforming love and power of Jesus till they are hoarse, but people are not going to listen very hard. There are a few churches in Britain that have learned this lesson. Their common life is so attractive and warm that outsiders are drawn to Jesus, and come to him whether or not the minister happens to be in residence. The work goes on without constant injections of life from the leadership. Because it is the life of the Body of Christ flowing out to folks in their need and loneliness. In churches like that men are daily added to the number of the believers just as they were in the first century. But let none of us think that we can "run" a church like that. It can only come as the Lord the Spirit is in control of ministers and people alike, as mutual trust grows among the members, and as the gifts of different members are recognized and given full play. Above all, Christians must be prepared to be honest with each other, and not keep up a facade of goodness. After all, we are accepted by God while we are sinners, and should not need to pretend to each other that we are anything different. When that costly "body life" is characteristic of modern Christianity, it may well have the same success as it did in the early centuries.

(ii) The value of *homes*. To be sure, the early Christians were driven to make a great deal of use of the home, because they were not allowed to possess any property until the end of the second century. They were not allowed to have large public meetings under the rule of a number of the emperors because of the possible political implications. In other words, the church in the first three centuries grew without the aid of two of our most prized tools: mass evangelism and evangelism in church. Instead, they used the home. In Acts we read of homes being used extensively, such as the homes of Jason and of Justus, of Philip and of Mark's mother. Sometimes it is a prayer meeting, sometimes an evening for fellowship and instruction, sometimes a Communion service, sometimes a meeting for new converts, sometimes a houseful of seekers, sometimes an impromptu gathering.

The value of the home as opposed to, or rather complementary to, the more formal worship in church, is obvious. It enables people to question (and check) the leader. It promotes dialogue. It enables difficulties to be sorted out. It facilitates fellowship. It can so easily issue in corporate action and service in which all the different limbs in the body can play their part. Of course, some clergy don't like it. It takes the power out of their hands; it can fragment the congregation; the groups can become introverted. All of these dangers are real. But they are dangers the early church managed to overcome, for the most part. And so can we . . . if we will trust the people of God to be the people of God in and through the home. The growing use of homes in Christian work the world over is one of the most encouraging signs of a breakthrough in evangelism in the future.

(iii) The use of *apologetic*. A marked feature of the early evangelists is that they used their minds to relate the Gospel to the intellectual and cultural concerns of their day. I am greatly impressed by the way the apologists of the second century continued as teachers of philosophy, convinced that they had found the true philosophy that would avail for all men anywhere. They related Christ to the intellectual world of their day, in terms which made sense to those who started with no Christian presuppositions. They set out to demonstrate the existence of the one God from whom everything derived. They laughed at the foolish polytheism of the Greek and Roman pantheon. They showed the folly of Homer and Hesiod in their popular epics, attributing human sins writ large to the gods, and instead pointed to the holiness of God, a holiness which struck a chord in every man's conscience. They argued the reality of the resurrection: Tertullian in his *de Resurrectione* maintains with good reason that if God could fashion a human body out of the fusion of sperm and egg, it is not in the least difficult to suppose that he could fashion a spiritual body for Christians in heaven, which would combine the continuity of the ego with a new and far more wonderful form for its expression. Origen's famous catechetical school at Alexandria was not only a training ground for Christian intellectuals, but a place where the faith was debated, argued over, and pressed home to sceptics and inquirers. It was the same 150 years earlier when Paul argued the Christian way against all comers at Tyrannus' school in Ephesus. The very words used in the New Testament to express the Christian preaching denote a high intellectual endeavor: words such as *didaskein*, "to instruct" *kerussein*, "to proclaim like a herald," *euangelizesthai*, "to proclaim good news," *katangellein*, "to make careful announcement," *diamarturesthai*, "to testify," *katelenchein*, "to convince by argument," *dialegesthai*, "to argue," and so forth. They spent a lot of time on this intellectual commendation of the Good News. They were prepared to argue, to go out on to neutral or hostile ground. They gave testimony, they had constant reference to the facts of the Gospel and the teaching of the Old Testament (words like *sunzetein* and *sumbibazein* indicate this serious searching of the Scriptures). Sometimes this took a day or even a week. Sometimes they returned to the attack again and again. But of the serious intellectual content of the proclamation in the early days, there can be no doubt. They would have gotten nowhere without such an apologetic. Both the Jewish and Gentile cultures were thoroughly opposed to what they had to tell. And if their position could be undermined by argument, they would soon have been driven off the streets. But it could not. It was the truth. And because it is the truth, followers of Christ need fear no truth, for it all belongs to him, and sheds some light on the truth made personal in Christ. It seems to me, therefore, that if we are to learn from the early Christians, we shall not be content with repeating louder and more often the "simple Gospel"; there is actually no such thing. For the truth is both so simple that a child can understand the bones of the matter, and so profound that no intellectual can ever plumb its depths. It is, of course, true that argument will never get a man into the Kingdom of God. The fact remains that many a man will never face up to the personal challenge of Jesus upon his life until he both sees an acceptable intellectual framework for belief, and has had his intellectual escape routes destroyed by a patient, efficient, convincing Christian apologetic. Men like Schaeffer, Guinness, and a few others are notable within our generation for attempting this most demanding intellectual and spiritual discipline of providing a Christian apologetic as a framework for proclaiming the Christian Gospel. We need a more widespread determination to follow their example if the Gospel is to be seen to be relevant to the intellectual as well as the cultural and moral needs of men. Personally, I always have a time for debate and questions in evangelistic work in universities throughout the world. I love meeting people in town halls, lecture theaters, dance halls, and pubs to debate the truth and the relevance of the Christian faith. I believe it is high time for us to emerge from the ghetto of intellectual obscurantism, just as we are beginning to emerge from the ghetto of evangelical shibboleths and church-building-centered ministry, on to the common ground, the neutral places, the places where men debate and congregate and argue. That is where the battle was won in the early days. Today, most of us have hardly begun to fight on this sort of ground.

(iv) I notice the priority of *personal conversation* among the early Christians. It was a method Jesus employed a great deal. St. John's Gospel has a particular interest in these personal encounters of Jesus with individuals, and the variety of approach he took with each of them, in every case finding a way to them through their felt need, and never bound to a system. It was Philip's way when he led the Ethiopian eunuch to Christ, Paul's way when he brought Onesimus to the faith. And so it continued. The personal witness of an old man who met him in the fields and brought the conversation around to Jesus marked the beginning of Justin's conversion, early in the second century. Cyprian was won through the personal conversation of a presbyter who visited him, Gregory through the personal work of Origen. There is a lovely passage at the beginning of Minucius Felix's *Octavius* which sheds a lot of light on the way these conversations might begin and be carried on, in this instance, along the seashore as two friends go for a walk.

Perhaps this is the greatest lesson we can learn from the early church in the very changed situation of our own day. The most effective method of evangelism and the most widespread, in the long run, in its results, is conversation evangelism, where one who has found Jesus shares his discovery, his problems, his joys and his sorrows with one who is still groping in the dark. There is no joy like introducing a friend to Christ in this way. You do not need to be clever or experienced. You do not need to be an eloquent speaker, or capable of arranging your material in an orderly fashion. You just need to love the Lord, love your friend, and talk to the one about the other, in prayerful dependence on the Spirit, and then to the other about the one whom you have found to be alive and able to transform you. If all Christians set about doing this, they would not need much other methodology from the early church. The Gospel would once more spread like wildfire.

3.
CONVERSION
STEPHEN C. NEILL

The duty of the Church to evangelise is now a commonplace of all ecumenical discussion. The moment, however, that we go beyond vague generalisation, it becomes apparent that there are within the Church widely divergent ideas as to what evangelism is, and as to how it ought to be carried out. This has proved in many places an insuperable obstacle to common planning and action.

At no point is this disagreement more apparent than on the question of conversion. Even the meeting of minds in rational discussion of the problem is not easy to achieve. To those who can look back on some recognisable experience of conversion in their own lives, this is so much more important than anything else that they find it very difficult to take seriously any type of Christian living from which this experience is eliminated. Those who have had no such experience tend to be unable to get beyond the idea that conversion is some kind of emotional experience, and are thus unable to enter into any serious discussion of the real questions involved.

One of our most urgent needs is a thorough, scientific and theological study of the whole subject in the light of modern psychological knowledge, and of the rediscovery of biblical theology. It is unfortunate that the classic work, from which almost all modern consideration of the topic starts, William James' *Varieties of Religious Experience*, has proved in some respects misleading. James really deals rather with one type of religious experience than with the possible varieties of experience, and within that one type rather with instances that are in some way abnormal than with those that can be classed as "normal", if that word can ever be used of any human being or any human experience.

It may help to clarify the issue, if we state in the extremest form two antithetic approaches to the problem, recognising that there is an element of exaggeration in the statements, and that each is open to criticism on various grounds:

(a) Conversion is the beginning of real Christian life. Christian nurture, education and worship may be valuable preparations. But no one is, or should be called, a Christian until he has personally encountered God in Jesus Christ,

until he has personally repented, until he has personally accepted God's gift of salvation through faith in Christ, until by this faith he has individually been born again. The reality of the Church in every generation consists in those who have thus been born again. The continuance of the Church in the world depends on there being enough people who have passed through this experience, and through whom it can be passed on to others.

(b) Christian life begins at baptism, when by the grace of God operating through the Church, original sin is taken away, and the divine life is sown as a seed in the heart of man. Through Christian teaching, through life in the Church and through the grace of the sacraments, this seed can grow. Though growth may be hindered by resistance on the part of the individual, nevertheless it is a continuous process. To demand any other decisive new beginning is to deny the reality of the grace of God. What the individual is called to do is to recognise the reality of what God has already done in him and to take that seriously.

In general, this second position, with considerable variations, is that maintained by the Roman Catholic and Orthodox Churches, and by the state Churches of Europe, where it is taken for granted that the normal sequence of Christian nurture, worship, special religious instruction and Confirmation will lead on to full membership and responsibility in the Church. The first position, again with many variations, is that maintained by the evangelical Free Churches, and by evangelical movements within the more traditional Churches. In one case membership in the Church is expected to lead on to personal Christian experience. In the other, personal Christian experience is regarded as the pre-condition for effective membership in the Church.

If conversion is not an emotional experience, what is it? The following statement might win fairly wide acceptance among those who "preach for conversion", and regard it as essential for all men, as a part of their Christian experience:

"Conversion is primarily an act of determination of the will. All men are in a state of alienation from God; each man is the centre of his own world, and claims the right to determine his own existence. This is rebellion and the way of death. Even those who have been baptised do in practice go on living in this way; particular sins are the fruit of the central sin of rebellion. Real life begins only when a man consciously finds his true centre in God. God's offer of grace in Christ is continuous and unconditional. But it constrains no man and leaves the freedom of decision to men. To return to God is response to the love of God manifest in Christ. Nevertheless it is impossible without a decision on the part of the individual, the exercise of that freedom which has been impaired by sin, but which God Himself has kept in being in every man. Without this personal and individual response, there can be no reality of Christian life."

Obviously, there will be immense varieties in the way in which individuals are brought to the point at which this response is possible. For some, the clearing away of a mass of prejudices and intellectual difficulties may be a necessary preliminary. Others may be so sunk in psychological entanglements that no real personal decision becomes possible until a measure of mental health has been restored. In some cases, conversion appears sudden, though in almost all such cases, examination will show that there has been a long period of inner preparation. In many cases, the occasion, by which the decision is determined and in relation to which it is made, may appear quite trivial. The immediate effect on moral character may be very marked, or almost imperceptible. The interpretation given of the experience may be determined much more by outside influences than by the experience itself. (Accounts of their conversion by converts from non-Christian religions are nearly always jejune, trite, and phrased in the current vernacular of the Christian body to which they have given their adherence.)

But, under all these varieties, there will always be found certain common traits in every genuine record of conversion:

There is at least a minimum intellectual content. No one can be converted to Jesus Christ, unless he has a mental picture of Jesus, which, however imperfectly, is related to the truth and the reality of Jesus.

But the central factor is always in the will. Conversion always involves acceptance of the will of God as that which determines the life of men, and this involves the repudiation of the old self-centred and self-determining will.

Emotion is largely irrelevant to the significance of conversion. It may be markedly present or it may not. The conversions which are most permanent are usually those in which the emotional element is least present. Strong emotion is dangerous, as it can easily disguise the ethical element which must be present in all genuine conversion, and may even be used as an evasion of the new orientation of the will. Misuse of the emotional appeal by unskilled evangelists has done more than anything else to confuse the issue, and to discredit the idea of conversion.

The results of any genuine conversion will always be found to include at least the following elements:

(a) The establishment of an I-Thou relationship between the soul of man and God. What had been external now has become genuinely inward and personal.

(b) A sense of God's favour revealed in Christ to the individual. This is based not on emotional feeling, but on the Word and promises of God.

(c) Submission to the will of God continually renewed, and with it the realisation of the living Christ as the inward power of the new life.

(d) Repentance and a new sense of ethical obligation.

(e) Acceptance of responsibility in and for the Christian fellowship. (Individualism is a characteristic of mysticism, and not of evangelical religion.)

(f) A serious acceptance of responsibility to bear witness and to win others for Christ. On this depends the naturally self-propagating character of the Christian fellowship.

Obviously in most cases the individual cannot be aware of all these things at the moment or in the experience of conversion. Much instruction may be needed to make plain to him all that is involved in what he has done. But all these things are implicit in the act of accepting Jesus Christ as Saviour and Lord, and no conversion can be accepted as genuine, unless all these consequences follow from what has been done.

Many problems remain still to be considered in this field. Space permits the mention of only two:

(a) What is to be thought of similar conversion experiences in non-Christian religions? (cf. A. D. Nock: *Conversion* and Underwood: *Conversion, Christian and non-Christian*). Is there any clear and valid distinction? The same problem arises in relation to mysticism, as represented in Hinduism, Sufism, etc., etc. The answer depends on the view taken of human experience and its relation to external reality; it cannot be determined by a study of psychological process. If experience is really experience of an external reality, then the nature of the experience is determined by that which it is an experience *of*. If Christian faith brings men into an I-Thou relationship with Jesus Christ, in that rests the distinctiveness of the experience and its incommensurability with every other.

(b) What is to be said of the fact that most experiences of conversion appear to take place during the troubled years of adolescence? Does not this indicate a serious danger of illusion, self-deception and instability in such experiences? Here much fuller study is needed than has yet been made. It may be pointed out however that the occurrence of such experiences mainly in the adolescent age-group is not in itself any ground for criticism or objection, since there is strong evidence that, in spite of the emotional instability of that period, it is in fact that part of life in which character is most rapidly being formed, and in which most of the decisions are taken which determine the future of the individual. It is interesting to note that the Roman Catholic Church, which more than any other tends to frown on the idea of conversion in the evangelical sense, ordinarily begins its training of boys for the priesthood at the age of seventeen, thus assuming that it is usual for "vocation" to be recognised precisely in the unstable years of adolescence.

The primary aim of this study is to bring out into clear light the differences between Christians who alike are sincerely seeking the glory of God and the good of the Church.

Here attention has been drawn to the differences as they present themselves in the context of practical action. But it will be found that differences of approach and method attach themselves to much deeper grounds of division—in the theology and ethos of the various confessions, and even in their basic apprehension of Christian faith. Such differences cannot be reconciled on the practical level. But if the study of evangelism is to wait upon their reconciliation, it will wait for a very long time. And, if it is recognised that Christian faith and action can only artificially be separated from one another, no harm is done by considering at what points in the field of evangelism and conversion closer understanding and co-operation can be reached.

When the differences are stated in an extreme form, it may seem difficult to find any points of agreement from which progress towards understanding may be made. This would be too pessimistic a conclusion. It does seem that, even when the differences are most categorically stated, there are two points in which all would be in agreement:

(a) Christian life, in whatever form, is always response to the gracious activity of God in Christ. The initiative always rests with God, who approaches man as Redeemer, and not with the individual, whatever his seeking and striving after God.

(b) Christian life cannot be other than an affair of decisions. God chooses to be the Saviour of man. But man also chooses to live as a son of God—or chooses to live otherwise. The nature of this choice may be variously interpreted. The point at which the choice is first made may be impossible to detect. Nevertheless, among the many choices and decisions made by one who lives as a Christian, there must be one choice and decision, which in fact was the first. And the first is always the most important, though its importance may not be recognised at the time.

In a full study, it would be necessary to pay attention to the problems of loss or temporary obscuration of faith, relapse, the persistence of sin, recidivism, and so forth. But as these are common to all parts of the Christian Church, and are not eliminated by any type of approach or understanding, they need be no more than indicated at this point.

Most of what has been written so far has dealt with the problem of conversion from the standpoint of countries in which the Christian tradition has been long established, and in which children are born into an existing Christian community. But it is widely recognised that a great deal of light is shed on the problems by the experiences of the Church in the non-Christian world, where the approach is to the individual entirely untouched by any Christian influences at all. These experiences become all the more important and relevant, since, in the West, the Church finds itself increasingly face to face with similar conditions. In some countries of Europe, only a small minority of the children are baptised; only a small minority receive any Christian instruction. The thinking of modern man is determined much more by pagan than by Christian categories. Even in those countries where the Christian tradition has been more strongly maintained, it is no longer possible to count, as it was until recently, on even an elementary acquaintance with the Bible or with the facts of the life of Christ. What do the problems of evangelism and of conversion look like in this new setting?

In all recent testimony from the "mission field", immense stress is laid on the part played in evangelism by the Christian community. It is the life and witness of the Christian community *as a community* that is the effective power in evangelism. The non-Christian, who in any way becomes interested in the Gospel, comes to understand something of the meaning of it not so much by an intellectual process of absorption, as by entering into the life of the Christian community, coming to feel as it feels, and gradually apprehending the vital forces which are at work in it as the body of Christ.

This is wholly true, but it cannot be taken as a complete statement of the case. Inquiry on a very wide scale among converts from non-Christian religions indicates that in a very large number of cases, what first attracted their attention was some action on the part of a Christian which presented itself as radically different from the kind of action which would have been taken by a non-Christian in similar circumstances (e.g. in the matter of true and false testimony in the law-courts, a perennial problem in non-Christian countries). The next step has in many cases been personal friendship with an individual Christian, who may or may not have borne direct testimony to Christ in words. Introduction to the fellowship of the Christian community has usually been the third, and not the first, stage of the process.

Integration into the Christian community is essential for the convert, since it is only in living within that community that he can learn what it really means to be a Christian. But once this is stated, two grave problems immediately arise:

(a) It is necessary for the convert to be fully integrated into the Christian community; otherwise his own Christian life does not develop as it should. But he should not be separated more than is absolutely necessary from the social milieu in which he has grown up; otherwise he becomes almost completely ineffective as a witness, and is in danger of becoming a stranger, living in two worlds in neither of which he is perfectly at home. This is, in an acute form, a tension which is always present in every form of Christian living. The Christian community must be separated from the world, otherwise it loses its divine character. The Church must not be separated from the world, otherwise it ceases to perform its function as light and salt. This tension will be with us till the end of time; there can never be more than approximate and partial solutions, and on this subject there can be legitimate differences between groups of Christians equally devoted and equally sincere.

(b) What is to be done, where there is no Christian community, into which the convert can be introduced, other than that of the professional Christian workers? This situation arises at the beginning of all successful missionary work. It is beginning to be recognised as a problem in the renewed penetration of the secularised world by the Gospel. To deny the convert the only fellowship available to him is impossible. To admit him to that fellowship may very quickly turn him into the typical pseudo-layman, the half-lay, half-clerical type which is specially offensive to the genuine layman. Again there is no immediate solution; the problem largely solves itself with the growth of a Christian community, deeply rooted in the local situation, and strong enough to have an independent life of its own.

This emphasis on the community and its part in evangelism is further borne out by the experience of the so-called Mass Movements, which have been taking place in many parts of the world, and particularly in India. In some forms of society, decisions are taken by the group rather than by the individual. In so important a matter as a change of religion, it seems natural in such a society that the unit of action should be the group. In various periods of Church history, we find a similar process at work. The conversion of the greater part of Europe was the result of mass movements of tribes rather than of the conversion of individuals.

Most missionaries now accept this argument as valid, and believe that such Mass Movements are a real movement of the Spirit of God. It is important, however, not to overlook the passionate opposition to the whole idea manifested by many of the most distinguished Indian leaders of the Church; their contention is that such movements can never lead to anything but a base mixture of Christianity and paganism, and that the low level of Christian life seen in Mass Movement communities will in the end prove one of the greatest possible hindrances to the final conversion of India to the Christian faith.

This is not the place for a discussion of this interesting divergence of view. A few special points, however, may be noted in passing.

We are faced here, in one of its sharpest forms, with the question as to the objective of the evangelist: should he try to detach individuals from the mass of non-Christian society by means of personal conversion? Or should he try to penetrate the whole of that non-Christian society with the Gospel, in the hope of producing a landslide later on?

This has for a very long time been a matter of debate in missionary circles in India. The time has now come when a verdict has been pronounced by the course of Christian history. It seems to be clear that those who have gone on the first line, of aiming at producing converts, have won (in most cases) a small number of converts, but have penetrated society far beyond the limits of the range of their immediate and effective action; whereas those who have followed the method of peaceful penetration have made no converts, and have penetrated society far less deeply than those whose evangelistic purpose has been more direct and aggressive. From this judgment of history, it may be possible to draw certain lessons from the Church in its present situation in the west.

Study of the history of Mass Movements shows that in no case do they take shape primarily as a sub-conscious movement in the common mind of a group. Every Mass Movement on record has taken its start from intense personal conviction on the part of an individual. This individual has frequently to undergo persecution as a disturber of the social order in which he has been born. Usually his progress in attaching adherents to his point of view is for a time extremely slow. (The history of Muhammad in Mecca is a most interesting non-Christian parallel.) The group movement follows only if the first converts remain firm in the face of all the opposition that befalls them. Even in primitive societies, where the influence of the group mind is at its strongest, the faculty of individual decision and action is never completely uninhibited. Any progress made by the group in the religious or in any other sphere, always can be traced back to the courage and initiative of an individual.

This fact does not provide us with any answer to the question of the detachment of the converted individual from his group. In non-Christian countries, baptism is usually taken much more seriously than in countries with a long Christian tradition. It is taken as seriously by the non-Christians as by the would-be Christians, and is taken as marking the definite detachment of the individual from his tribe or caste. Wise strategy in mission fields has usually suggested the delaying of baptism as long as possible, in the hope that the converts may remain within their social group, until they have won the whole of it to the faith, and so avoid the schism which often does take place when one part of the group becomes Christian and another remains pagan. But sooner or later, and often sooner, the point comes at which a break must be made. Unless the Christians are in a position in which they can show their own distinctiveness in relation to such matters as participation in social customs of a pagan kind, they tend to lose their own fervour of conviction, and their power to influence. By delaying too long the decision of the individual for the sake of the group, it is possible to lose both the individual and the group. At no point can the individual factor in conversion be eliminated.

The great danger in all group movements is that adhesion to the new, or to the transformed, group, may be taken as a substitute for personal confrontation with Christ. Every missionary is well aware of the addiction of the inquirer to finding substitutes, by the acceptance of which he can evade the painfulness of real Christian decision. It is well known that Mass Movements, unless very carefully developed, tend to lose their force and die away within a generation. What is the reason for this? If hundreds and thousands of people are admitted in a comparatively short time to the Christian Church, intense spiritual effort must be applied to the care of them for a very long time. Otherwise the result is a large nominally Christian population, with no apparent desire for further spiritual progress, and living on so low a level of Christian achievement as to be a hindrance to any further progress of the Gospel among the non-Christians living round about it. Again we are forced back to the individual. If in a mass movement area a sufficient number of people are led to personal surrender to Christ and to the transformation of personality which follows from it, the movement will remain in motion. These living individuals are the centres of radiation throughout the Christian community and beyond it. If such individuals are too few or non-existent, the movement becomes stagnant and may develop from an opportunity to a menace.

In this brief study, it has not been possible to argue any point at length. For the sake of brevity, the form of statement has had to be dogmatic. The aim throughout has been to throw problems into relief, and to indicate some of the sources from which further light may be sought, and some of the answers which may provisionally be given. At every point, the need has been felt for a far more extensive and deeper study than, as far as the writer is aware, has been made in recent times. This study is not academic. The answers given to the questions raised will affect the whole approach of the Church to its evangelistic task. There must always be room for wide diversity of interpretation and approach. But unless there is agreement on a common aim, mutual understanding and, still more, common action, become impossible. We are always lamenting that the disunity of the Church is one of the chief causes of its weakness in the modern world. United evangelism is often proclaimed as one of the points at which the Church can recover its lost unity. Is this true? Or is a difference about the nature and purpose of evangelism just one of those points at which the helpless dividedness of the Church is most clearly brought into view?

---

[1] This "Introductory Statement" was prepared for the Conference on "The Evangelisation of Man in Modern Mass Society", held at Oxford last year, under the auspices of the Study Department of the World Council of Churches.

4.
THE NEW BIRTH

L. HAROLD DEWOLF

A. NECESSITY OF THE NEW BIRTH
1. Salvation and Our Human Predicament

The Christian gospel is good news of salvation. Salvation is the being saved from bondage to sin and entering into the eternal community of love under the reign of God. Salvation thus involves change within the individual, change in his relation to God and change in his relation to other persons.

We have seen how deeply every human person is caught in a network of evil constraints from his birth. He is not satisifed to live under them and yet he has inadequate power to overcome them so long as he seeks to do so in his own strength. For actually he has not the power to live at all in his own strength and so long as he tries to do so he is basing his conduct on a false construction of his whole situation. From the very root of his being he is dependent on other human persons and absolutely dependent upon God. Every true growth and every victory of his spiritual life must occur in willing acceptance of this relationship to God and to human society.

But his dependence upon his fellows deepens his problem. For human society is deeply infected with sinful motives and customs and many of its institutions are hardened channels of evil. Sometimes, seeing how dependent we are upon the family, church, state, economic order and other institutions, and how potent they are in forming our very souls, we are tempted to think that all would be well if only the institutional forms of our interpersonal relations were set right. Certainly no life can be fully victorious over sin without in some way challenging and combating the institutional evils which cramp and pervert many of our relations with one another. But institutional change alone is shown by experience to be short-lived and futile. The most admirable political constitution can be debased to serve the most unjust and tyrannical purposes. The finest economic organization can be used for the vilest exploitation. Even a church, committed formally to the highest ideals of purity and brotherly love, can be made the cloak for lewd practices or the cruelest racism. Not only the forms of an institution, but also the persons who control it, must be fit if the institution is actually to support justice and right.

2. "You Must be Born Anew"

Some theologians have written as if salvation were only a kind of heavenly legal transaction in which God came to treat as righteous persons, sinners who still continued, unchanged, in their sin. It is, indeed, hard to overestimate the importance of divine forgiveness in the work of salvation. But to deny or minimize the real change of life which is brought about here and now in the man who turns to God in faith and is received into His fellowship is to alter almost beyond recognition the teaching of the New Testament and also to deny the witness of a great multitude of men and women, many of whose changed lives can be observed in the present generation. The gospel message does not offer justification in continuing sinfulness, but summons the reader to

> be transformed by the renewal of your mind, that you may prove what is that good and acceptable and perfect will of God.[1]

This transformation is essential to life in fellowship with God. God loves and seeks all men. But the riches of His peace can be shared only with those who, being saved from bondage to sin, seek to participate in His purpose. This is not because of some arbitrary requirement of God external to our nature, but because we are created for this obedient participation and can find wholeness of our own spirits on no other terms. Hence, seeing that we have all, in a sinful society, fallen under the power of sin, it is true of every man that "unless one is born anew, he cannot see the kingdom of God."[2]

But what of the person who "grows up in the Christian faith"? If his life from the beginning is nurtured by Christian parents in the knowledge and love of god, must he still undergo a cataclysmic new birth?

In the account of Jesus' warning to Nicodemus about the necessity of the new birth, we are told, Nicodemus was perplexed and Jesus after reaffirming the necessity, added:

> Do not marvel that I said to you, "You must be born anew." The wind blows where it wills, and you hear the sound of it, but you do not know whence it comes or whither it goes; so it is with every one who is born of the spirit.[3]

The spiritual rebirth must come if the life in communion with God is to be entered. *How* it is to come cannot be determined by any formula. We cannot say when or how fast everyone must be reborn. Neither can we say that in everyone the new birth will appear as a radical reversal of direction. The Spirit works in many different ways in different lives.

But let no one say that because the change may occur slowly or in the secrecy of the heart it need not occur at all. For if the soul is to enter into communion with God, there must come sometime somehow the awakening to solemn responsibility before God and the commitment of the soul to side with Him and by His grace to wage unceasing war against evil in the self and in the world.

Nicodemus was not the last man to be puzzled about the meaning of this doctrine of the new birth. It is still a subject of much perplexity and no little controversy. The theologian must make some attempt to find and expound as clearly as possible the truth to be discovered in this teaching. The whole truth that is discoverable will be seen to exceed by far the limits of psychological or of ethical description. Yet the categories of psychology and of ethics do provide useful vehicles for empirical approaches particularly relevant to present thought. We begin with the approach of psychology.

B. SECOND BIRTH PSYCHOLOGICALLY DESCRIBED

1. Release from Symptoms of Guilt

A number of psychologists have described the alleviation or removal of guilt feelings occurring at many conversions.[4] Usually the subjects of such studies have been persons who experienced sudden and dramatic change. This is natural, for the data in such cases are especially conspicuous and easily contrasted. However, the release from consciously felt or long-repressed guilt conflicts is often as great or greater in cases where the changes are slower and less exposed to the public eye.

2. Change in Capacity for Other-Concern

A person who was formerly full of fear, anxiety, self-pity and other forms of preoccupation with himself is often observed to have gained confidence and security, through his conversion, and to have turned attention outward in active, sympathetic concern for other persons. By "finding God" many people have been quite observably turned from ingrown self-concern to a genuine interest in the needs of others and to co-operative participation in unselfish benevolence.

3. Change in Gallery

We sometimes speak contemptuously of the person who "plays to the gallery" or to "the stands." He prefers the plaudits of the crowd, we think, rather than genuine achievement or qualitative superiority. He seeks the spotlight, the spectacular play, the solo performance. But if we suppose that his fault is in caring for the high valuation by other persons, in contrast to the admirable people who do not care, we are quite mistaken. For every one of us is so completely social in nature that none can avoid a concern for the approval of others. In hours of decision we can all observe our own concern to know how such and such persons would think of us if we made the choice contemplated. We can, however, choose our galleries. The athlete can have a higher regard for the approval of the experts, of his teammates and of his coach than for the applause of superficial and untrained spectators.

Augustine turns, at conversion, from striving to please sophisticated pagans to the effort to please the most thoughtful Christians, especially his mother, but above all to please God. So also the writer of the Letter to the Hebrews calls before the reader one after another of the great heroes of faith and then declares,

Therefore, since we are surrounded by so great a cloud of witnesses, let us lay aside every weight, and sin which clings so closely, and let us run with perseverance the race that is set before us, looking to Jesus, the pioneer and perfecter of our faith. . . . [5]

So Paul reminds the Christians of Thessalonica that they have learned from him how they "ought to live and to please God." [6] The direction of movement in any life depends largely on the secret gallery which he carries within his own soul. So it is a matter of no small import, when a man accepts for his "witnesses" pre-eminent exemplars of Christian virtues, with Jesus Christ at the head, and seeks above all "to please God."

4. Change in Ego-Identification

Everyone carries in his own mind a certain impression of the kind of person he is or means to be. This impression is often far different from the view which his friends and neighbors have of him and it may be far from the reality. But it does profoundly affect what he is becoming.

A youth of seventeen wandered into a city mission one evening looking for food and shelter. He had left his home and school several years earlier and was as aimless a wanderer as one could find. In response to every effort to portray the possibilities of a more meaningful life, he replied that he could not do anything, that he was "no good" or that he had "no will power." He had never received any religious instruction and all he knew about the name "Jesus Christ" was that it was "swear words." Yet after he had been prevailed upon to stay at the mission for a few days some appeal reached him, one evening, and he went to the altar seeking God. When he arose from his knees that night he had a new conception of himself. From that day he set out quietly and confidently to do the things he had been sure he could not do—quitting strong drink, seeking and achieving reconciliation with his parents, studying conscientiously, obtaining and successfully holding a job. Until that night he had been in his own eyes a bum. Now he was, in his own eyes, a "saved" man, a Christian who could do everything God wanted him to do because God gave him the strength he had not possessed before.[7]

The psychologist, as psychologist, can observe and describe such changes. The description leaves many questions unanswered, particularly questions about the value of the changes and questions about their real *cause*. But when such problems are investigated psychology has been left behind. For example, when we ask whether the changes are for the better or worse and why, we enter the domain of ethics.

C. SECOND BIRTH ETHICALLY DESCRIBED

1. Narrowing the Gap between Ideals and Conduct

The youth who first stumbled into the mission dismally condemned himself. His ideals, that is, the types of conduct which he approved, were quite contrary to the mode of life which he daily lived. Yet he was doing nothing to close the gap.

This is precisely the condition of will which is most surely condemned by the ethical theory of many schools. For no matter what criterion of moral judgment may be defended and no matter what the supreme good of life is taken to be, the violation of one's own accepted standards is bound to be self-defeating.

Hence the great increase in self-mastery, enabling the youth to set his direction of development firmly toward his own ideals, was in itself, at least, morally all to the good.

2. Overcoming of Conflict in Ideals

Part of the difficulty which the sinner experiences in trying to live up to his ideals is due to the fact that his ideals themselves conflict. For example, if he approves both a sober life of achievement and also an accepted place in a group of irresponsible drifters or when he favors both brotherhood and the making of the most money possible, he is doomed to internal conflict of will. When such a person settles once and for all the question of his supreme allegiance so that all else must then be subject to the one organizing principle, that does not resolve for him the countless perplexities and struggles over the means which should be adopted in the various situations of life. But it does resolve the deeper and far more disruptive conflicts over the basic purposes and goals of life.

The student of ethics can observe such integrating organization of ideals in the life of the man who gives himself to God as revealed in Jesus Christ.

3. Change to More Inclusive Loyalties

Increased breadth of view is likewise typical of conversion experience. The central principle of organization which brings unity to the ideals of the twice-born requires also a concern as wide as the concern of God is believed to be. Since God, according to Christian teaching, created all men and Christ gave his life for all, this concern is, in principle, universal in scope. The restricting temptations of selfishness and every type of provincialism still confront the converted person. Individuals and whole churches frequently succumb to them. But Christian conversion sets at the heart of the believer an inclusive loyalty which puts all lesser, exclusive devotions on the defensive.

From the standpoint of a rational ethics, this is worthy of approval. The wider the range of perspective taken into account in establishing ideals and determining conduct, the greater the likelihood of eventual subjective and social consistency and harmony.[8]

Specifically, the ideal of what human personality ought to become, as seen in Jesus Christ, gives to the converted person a concrete and superb goal of individual life. Similarly, the ideal of the perfect community taught in his doctrine of the kingdom of heaven and supported by experiences of Christian fellowship, provides an exacting and persuasive norm for the judging and development of all social relationship. Both of these ideals are sufficiently defined in New Testament teaching and narrative and sufficiently concrete in the Christian's experience, to have an appeal which no abstract concept could possess. Yet they also leave adequate scope for creative adaptation to ever-changing circumstances and needs.

But however highly the ethical theorist may approve the ideals and even the moral progress of the convert, he can hardly answer, as ethical theorist, the crucial questions concerning the new birth. For these questions would seek explanation of the power which enables the subject to close the gap between ideals and conduct and the experience because of which God and His kingdom are living realities and not abstract ideals to the transformed person. The raising of such questions, as well as some approached by the psychologist, demand religious or theological description for answer.

D. THE NEW BIRTH THEOLOGICALLY DESCRIBED

1. Repentance

Near the beginning of the Gospel accounts comes the story of John the Baptist with his warning demand that his hearers repent of their sins. In the Lord's Prayer, no sooner do we ask for the coming of the kingdom, the doing of God's will on earth and the providing of our daily bread than we are reminded of our own unworthiness to receive such blessings. Therefore, we must hasten to add, "Forgive us . . . " Over and over again, in the sermons of the earliest Christian preachers we read the call to repentance:

Repent, and be baptized every one of you in the name of Jesus Christ for the forgiveness of your sins.[9]

Repent therefore, and turn again, that your sins may be blotted out.[10]

The times of ignorance God overlooked, but now he commands all men everywhere to repent.[11]

So near is this to the heart of Paul's message that he describes his work as a declaring to both Jews and Gentiles "that they should repent and turn to God and perform deeds worthy of repentance."[12]

This is the starting point of the decisive transaction between the individual soul and God. God is righteous and true fellowship between Him and the sinner is impossible until the sinner repents.

Yet this is not the first beginning. A man cannot repent until he is moved to be sorry for his transgressions and until he has hope of forgiveness. This sorrow and this hope God has prepared through all His beneficence to the sinner, through every human kindness to him and through his life, death and resurrection of Christ. Through all these instruments the Holy Spirit now moves the heart to repentance. When the burdened heart responds with its plea for forgiveness, the way is opened for the new relationship.

This repentance must be a whole-response of faith. It will not do to select a sin or two, here or there, and ask that these be forgiven. When repentance is genuine it always does include some specific wrongs. But the sinner—anyone—who would enter into life-giving communion with God must ask the forgiveness of any and all mistakes, sins and social involvements which stand as barriers to this communion.

2. Forgiveness by God

"If we confess our sins, he is faithful and just, and will forgive our sins and cleanse us from all unrighteousness."[13] God's merciful readiness to forgive us is sure. We can be confident that when we wholeheartedly repent He does forgive.

But there is a pitfall here against which warning must be often repeated. Being sure that when we repent God does forgive, we may then think of our repentances as the important thing. Then the forgiveness is so taken for granted as to be easily forgotten. When that attitude prevails the "repentance" becomes only a subjective self-treatment, losing its character of confession and appeal to the true Father whose forgiveness we need. If the confession is to be genuine it must be truly personal, a prayer to the one who is "faithful and just," but to whom we should therefore all the more look with wonder and gratitude and least of all take lightly for granted.

3. Receiving God's Grace to Do His Will

With God's forgiveness there is given new strength to overcome the old temptations and to do what was previously impossible. Before this, any sinner could testify,

> I do not understand my own actions. For I do not do what I want, but I do the very thing I hate.... I can will what is right, but I cannot do it. For I do not do the good I want, but the evil I do not want is what I do.[14]

But when God has done his transforming work there is a quite different testimony to make. "For the law of the Spirit of life in Christ Jesus has set me free from the law of sin and death."[15] Those who seek complete and final explanation of this change of life in the psychological forces within the man himself miss both the secret of explanation and the message of hope to be given other burdened spirits. For the change in the self is brought about in an encounter with the one Other who is able to forgive all sin and to set men "free from the law of sin and death."

How God performs this change in us, we do not fully understand. We can see many of the instruments He employs—the psychological and ethical descriptions have suggested some of them—but much we know simply as His work, just as we know that He has created us and not we ourselves, but without our understanding how He creates. This new expansion of our freedom, is, indeed, a new going forth in us of His creative Word.

4. Entering the New Community

The new influx of spiritual strength does not end with the new birth. For that is but the beginning of a new relationship in which there is ever-renewed communion between God and a man, with God giving the support of His presence and love and with the man responding by an eager seeking of the divine will and by earnest, obedient faithfulness. The man, it is true, remains in the world and many influences press upon him to turn him away from God. But even though he sometimes falls before these temptations, he is quick to seek again the forgiveness of God, renewing the communion by which he lives. The center of power in his life and hence the direction of his development are now controlled by the divine-human relationship.

At the same time he has entered "the communion of saints," the comradeship of the spirit with a host of others who have entered into communion with God. This comradeship includes the "cloud of witnesses" whose work on earth is done. But it includes also the living company of pilgrims of the way. By this company he is sustained and encouraged in his spiritual growth and to it he contributes his own witness of faith and life.

E. FAITH AND WORKS IN SALVATION

The term "salvation" is sometimes used of the single transaction and change which has been here described as the new birth. More properly salvation includes not only the new birth, but the entire process of change and growth from sin to righteous perfection—a process beginning with the first stirrings of spiritual concern, before the new birth has taken place, and continuing on after death.

An old question is the problem of the roles played by faith and works in this process of salvation. There have been those who have denied that works had any place in the process at all. Likewise some, though fewer within the

Christian churches, have denied that faith had any place. These denials have often been due in whole or in part to a narrow definition of "works" as formally prescribed ritualistic acts or ascetic practices or a similarly narrow conception of "faith" as a mere assent to a creedal formula. When the opposite denials are based on such definitions they turn out to be strikingly similar in actual meaning, since both are then directed against the notion that God is concerned with our formal compliance with empty, legalistic prescriptions.

In the New Testament both faith and works, more broadly conceived, are given great prominence. In the Synoptic Gospels Jesus' stress seems to be well divided between works and love[16] and an attitude of trusting obedience in relation to the Father.[17] Since he teaches that God commands love toward Him and one's neighbor, the two strands of emphasis come out practically together. In the Johannine writings faith, with stress on right belief, is given greater emphasis,[18] along with the necessity of a spiritual union with Christ—as of the branches with a vine.[19]

It is, of course, in the letters of Paul and James that the issue is most precisely joined. "For we hold," says Paul, "that a man is justified by faith apart from works of law."[20] James, on the other hand, writes,

> What does it profit, my brethren, if a man says he has faith but has not works? Can his faith save him? If a brother or sister is ill-clad and in lack of daily food, and one of you says to them, "Go in peace, be warmed and filled," without giving them the things needed for the body, what does it profit? So faith by itself, if it has no works, is dead.[21]

Now it is apparent that in speaking of "works" Paul has at the center of his thought the formal requirements of the Jewish law. James, on the other hand, is speaking of the deeds which faith, if it is alive, is bound to produce. The central problem and the situation being different, the two writers use different emphasis. But when each comes to a balanced statement of his view, they speak alike. Thus Paul insists that all who have saving faith are bound to obey God,[22] while James declares, "Show me your faith apart from your works, and I by my works will show you my faith."[23]

The faith by which we are brought into a saving relation with God is evidently not a mere intellectual assent to a creed. "Even the demons believe," says James, "—and shudder."[24] We are saved by belief in a Person, not mere belief in a proposition. Such belief in God implies, of course, assent to the doctrine that He is and that He is worthy of our faith. But it includes also the attitude of trust and loyal obedience. It is not mere assent by faithfulness.[25]

When faith is understood, certainly it is by faith that we are saved. It is not by performing a certain number of religious chores, not even by giving to God a large number of acts, however good in themselves, regarded simply as means of purchasing our salvation. For salvation is no more to be purchased than is life itself. God alone can grant to us His saving love. And His love is not given to this or that act, but to whole persons. It is our very selves which must be committed to life with Him if we are to have such life. That whole commitment of ourselves into His hands is faith.

FOOTNOTES

[1] Rom. 12:2 (RSV marginal reading).
[2] Jn. 3:3.
[3] Jn. 3:5-8.
[4] E.g., see William James, *Varieties of Religious Experience*; J. B. Pratt, *The Religious Consciousness*; Edwin D. Starbuck, *The Psychology of Religion*; W. B. Thomas, *Psychology of Conversion*; and Paul E. Johnson, *Psychology of Religion*.
[5] Heb. 12:1-2.
[6] I Thess. 4:1. Cf. Rom. 8:8; I Cor. 7:32-34; Gal. 1:10; I Thess. 2:15.
[7] This is a factual account of events which I observed.
[8] Cf. "The Law of the Most Inclusive End" in E. S. Brightman, *Moral Laws*.
[9] Acts 2:38.
[10] Acts 3:19.
[11] Acts 17:30.
[12] Acts 26:19-20.
[13] I Jn. 1:9.
[14] Rom. 7:15, 18-19.
[15] Rom. 8:2-4.
[16] E.g., see Mt. 25-31-46; Mk. 10:17-21; Lk. 6:46-49.
[17] E.g., see Mt. 6:25-34.
[18] See, e.g., Jn. 8:24; I Jn. 4:2.
[19] Jn. 15:1-6.
[20] Rom. 3:28.
[21] Jas. 2:14-17.
[22] Rom. 6:12-19.
[23] Jas. 2:18.
[24] Jas. 2:19.
[25] Cf. Georgia Harkness' contrast between the near-universality of Americans' belief that God exists and the great number of these "believers" who live as if He did not. *The Modern Ritual of Christian Faith*, pp. 11-12.

5.
THE HIGHEST PRIORITY: CROSS-CULTURAL EVANGELISM

RALPH D. WINTER

The "really horrifying fact," according to Ralph D. Winter, is that "the vast bulk of evangelistic efforts, even missionary activities today, are caught-up in the internal affairs of the various church movements," leaving four out of five non-Christians in the world "beyond the reach of the ordinary evangelism of existing Christian churches." This situation requires, in his view, a re-ordering of priorities and a renewal of emphasis on *cross-cultural* evangelism because "most non-Christians . . . are not culturally near-neighbors of any Christians." Dr. Winter discusses a short-hand terminology (E-0, E-1, E-2, E-3) that he has developed for describing the "different kinds of evangelism" in terms of cultural distance and difficulty involved. He concludes that despite the "wonderful fact that there are now Christians throughout the whole world," cross-cultural evangelistic "efforts coming from outside are still essential and highly urgent," whether from the Western world or not. A former United Presbyterian missionary to Guatemala, Dr. Winter is now professor of the historical development of the Christian movement, School of World Mission at Fuller Theological Seminary, Pasadena, California. Dr. Winter edited this abridged version of the two papers he had prepared for the 1974 International Congress on World Evangelization at Lausanne. The full text of the two papers is published in *Let the Earth Hear His Voice*, edited by J. D. Douglas (Minneapolis: World Wide Publications, 1975), or is available as a booklet, *The New Macedonia*, from the William Carey Library, South Pasadena, California.

In recent years a serious misunderstanding has crept into the thinking of many evangelicals. Curiously it is based on a number of wonderful facts: the Gospel has now gone to the ends of the earth. Christians have now fulfilled the Great Commission in at least a geographical sense. At this moment of history we can acknowledge with great respect and pride those evangelists of every nation who have gone before us and whose sacrificial efforts and heroic accomplishments have made Christianity by far the world's largest and most wide-spread religion, with a Christian church on every continent and in practically every country. This is no hollow victory. Now more than at any time since Jesus walked the shores of Galilee, we know with complete confidence that the Gospel is for everyone, that it makes sense in any language and that it is not merely a religion of the Mediterranean or of the West.

This is all true. On the other hand many, many Christians have as a result of all this gotten the impression that the job is now nearly done and that to finish it we need only to forge ahead in local evangelism, reaching out wherever the new worldwide church has already been planted. Many Christian organizations, ranging from the World Council of Churches to many U.S. denominations and even some evangelical groups have thus rushed to the conclusion that we may now abandon traditional missionary strategy and simply count on local Christians everywhere to finish the job.

While most conversions must inevitably take place as the result of some Christian witnessing to a near neighbor—and that is evangelism—*the awesome fact is that most non-Christians in the world today are not culturally near-neighbors of any Christians, and it will take a special kind of "cross-cultural" evangelism to reach them.*

Consider the great Batak Church in Northern Sumatra. Here is one of the famous churches of Indonesia. Its members have been doing much evangelism among fellow Bataks of whom there are still many thousands whom they can reach without learning a foreign language, and among whom they can work with the maximum efficiency of direct contact and understanding. Even so, the majority of the people in Indonesia speak other languages and are of other ethnic units. Thus, for the Batak Christians of Northern Sumatra to win people to Christ in other parts of Indonesia is not the same as winning culturally near-neighbors. It is a distinctly different kind of task. It is another kind of evangelism—cross-cultural evangelism.

Or take the great church of Nagaland in Northeast India. Years ago American missionaries from the plains of Assam reached up into the Naga hills and won some of the Ao Nagas. Then these Ao Nagas won practically their whole tribe to Christ. Next, Ao Nagas won members of the nearby Santdam Naga tribe, who spoke a sister language. These new Santdam Naga Christians then proceeded to win almost the whole of their tribe. This process went on until the majority of all fourteen Naga tribes became Christian. Now that most of Nagaland is Christian—even the officials of the state government are Christian—there is the desire to witness elsewhere in India. But for these Nagaland Christians to win other people in India is as much a foreign mission task as it is for Englishmen, Koreans, or Brazilians to evangelize in India. This is one very substantial reason why, so far, the Nagas have made no significant attempt to evangelize the rest of India. India citizenship is indeed one advantage the Naga Christians have as compared with people from other countries, but citizenship does not make it easier for them to learn any of the hundreds of totally foreign languages in the rest of India.

In other words, if Nagas decide to evangelize other peoples in India they will need to employ a radically different kind of evangelism. The easiest kind, when they used their own language to win their own people, is now mainly in the past. A second kind of evangelism was not a great deal more difficult—where they won people of neighboring Naga tribes, whose languages were sister languages. A third kind of evangelism, needed to win people in far-off parts of India, will be much more difficult.

Let's give labels to these different kinds of evangelism. Where an Ao Naga won another Ao, let us call that *E-1 evangelism*. When an Ao went across a tribal language boundary to a sister language and won the Santdam, we'll call that task *E-2 evangelism*. (This E-2 task is not as easy and requires different techniques.) But then if an Ao Naga goes to another region of India, to a strange language such as Telegu, Korhu or Bhili, his task will be considerably more difficult than E-1 or even E-2 evangelism. We will call it *E-3 evangelism*. Note that we are classifying both E-2 and E-3 as *cross-cultural evangelism*.

Let us try out this terminology in another country. Take Taiwan. There are also different kinds of people there. The majority are Minnans who were there before a flood of Mandarin-speaking people came across from the mainland. Then there is the bloc of Hakka-speaking people who came from the mainland much earlier. Up in the mountains a few hundred thousand aboriginal peoples speak Malayo-Polynesian dialects entirely different from Chinese. Now if a mainland Chinese Christian wins others of his own kind that's E-1 evangelism. If he wins a Minnan Taiwanese or a Hakka, that's E-2 evangelism. If he wins someone from the hill tribes, that's E-3 evangelism.

Thus far we have referred only to language differences, but for the purpose of defining evangelistic strategy, any kind of obstacle, any kind of communication barrier affecting evangelism is significant. In Japan for example practically everybody speaks Japanese and there aren't radically different dialects of Japanese comparable to the different dialects of Chinese. But there are highly significant social differences that make it difficult for people from one group to win others of a different social class. In Japan as in India social differences often turn out to be more important in evangelism than language differences. Japanese Christians thus have not only an E-1 sphere of contact, but also E-2 spheres that are harder to reach. Japanese missionaries going from Japan to other parts of the world to work with non-Japanese with totally different languages are doing an evangelistic task on the E-3 level.

Finally, let me give an example from my own experience. I speak English as my native language. For ten years I lived and worked in Central America, most of the time in Guatemala, where Spanish is the official language, but where a majority of the people speak some dialects of the Mayan family of aboriginal languages. I had two languages to learn. Spanish has a 60 per cent overlap in vocabulary with English, so I had no trouble learning that language. Along with learning Spanish, I became familiar with the extension of European culture into the New World, and it was not particulary difficult to understand the lifeways of the kind of people who spoke Spanish. However, because Spanish was so easy by comparison, learning the Mayan language in our area was, I found, enormously more difficult. In our daily work switching from English to Spanish to a Mayan language made me quite aware of the three different "cultural distances." When I spoke of Christ to an American Peace Corps worker in English, I was doing E-1 evangelism. When I spoke to a Guatemalan in Spanish, it was E-2 evangelism. When I spoke to an Indian in the Mayan language, it was the even more difficult E-3 evangelism.

Everyone has his own E-1 sphere in which he or she speaks his or her own language and builds on all the intuition that derives from his experience within his or her own culture. Evangelism in such a sphere is not cross-cultural. Then, for almost all of us there is an E-2 sphere—groups of people who speak languages that are a little different, or who are involved in culture patterns sufficiently in contrast to our own to make communication more difficult and a separate congregational life desirable. Such people can be reached with a little extra trouble and with sincere attempts, but it will take us out of our way to reach them. *More important, they are people who, once converted, will not feel at home in the Church we attend.* In fact, they may grow faster spiritually if they can find Christian fellowship among people of their own kind. More significant to evangelism: it is quite possible that in a separate fellowship of their own they are more likely to win others of their own social sphere. That is, we must reach them by E-2 methods in order to enable them to win others by E-1 methods. Each of us has an E-3 sphere: most languages and cultures of the world are totally strange to us; they are at the maximum cultural distance. If we attempt to evangelize at this E-3 distance we have a long uphill climb in order to be able to make sense to anyone.

In summary, the master pattern of the expansion of the Christian movement is first for special E-2 and E-3 efforts to cross cultural barriers into new communities and to establish strong, on-going, vigorously evangelizing local churches and denominations, and then for that new "national" church to carry the work forward on the really high-powered E-1 level. We are thus forced to believe that until every tribe and tongue has a strong powerfully evangelizing church in it and thus an E-1 witness within it, E-2 and E-3 efforts coming from outside are still essential and highly urgent.

In view of the profound truth that (other things being equal) E-1 evangelism is more powerful than E-2 or E-3 evangelism, it is easy to see how some people have erroneously concluded that E-3 evangelism is therefore out of date, simply due to the wonderful fact that there are now Christians throughout the world. It is with this perspective that major denominations in the U.S. have at some points acted on the premise that there is no more need for missionaries of the kind who leave home to go to a foreign country and struggle with a totally strange language and culture. Their premise is that "there are Christians over there already." With the drastic fall-off in the value of the U.S. dollar and the tragic shrinking of many U.S. church budgets, some U.S. denominations have had to curtail their missionary activity to an astonishing extent, and they have in part tried to console themselves by saying that it is time for the national church to take over. In our response to this situation, we must happily agree that wherever there are local Christians effectively evangelizing there is nothing more potent than E-1 evangelism.

However, the truth about the superior power of E-1 evangelism must not obscure the obvious fact that E-1 evangelism is literally *impossible* where there are as yet no witnesses within a given language or cultural group. Jesus, as a Jew, would not have had to witness directly to that Samaritan woman had there been a local Samaritan Christian who had already reached her. In the case of the Ethiopian eunuch, we can conjecture that it might have been better for an Ethiopian Christian than for Philip to do the witnessing, but there had to be an initial contact by a non-Ethiopian in order for the E-1 process to be set in motion. This kind of initial multiplying work is the primary task of the missionary when he rightly understands his job. Hopefully Jesus' E-2 witness set in motion E-1 witnessing in that Samaritan town. Hopefully Philip's E-2 witness to the Ethiopian set in motion E-1 witnessing back in Ethiopia. If, for example, that Ethiopian was an Ethiopian Jew, the E-1 community back in Ethiopia might not have been very large and might not have effectively reached the non-Jewish Ethiopians. As a matter of fact, scholars believe that the Ethiopian Church today is the result of a much later missionary thrust that reached, by E-3 evangelism, the ethnic Ethiopians.

Unfortunately, most Christians have only a foggy idea of just how many different peoples there are in the world among whom there is no E-1 witness. But several recent studies have seriously raised this question: Are there any tribal tongues and linguistic units that have not yet been penetrated by the Gospel? If so, where and how many? Who can reach them? Even these preliminary studies indicate that cross-cultural evangelism must still be the highest priority. Far from being a task that is now out of date, the shattering truth is that at least four out of five non-Christians in the world today are beyond the reach of *any* E-1 evangelism.

Why is this fact not more widely known? I am afraid that all our exultation about the fact that every *country* of the world has been penetrated has allowed many to suppose that every *culture* has been penetrated. This misunderstanding is a malady so widespread that it deserves a special name. Let us call it "people blindness," that is blindness to the existence of separate peoples within *countries*. This is a blindness I might add that seems more prevalent in the U.S. and among U.S. missionaries than anywhere else. The Bible rightly translated could have made this plain to us. The "nations" to which Jesus often referred were mainly ethnic groups within the single political structure of the Roman government. The various nations represented on the day of the Pentecost were for the most part not *countries* but *peoples*. In the Great Commission as it is found in Matthew, the phrase "make disciples of all *ethne* (peoples)" does not end our responsibility once we have a church in every country—God wants a strong church within every people!

"People blindness" is what prevents us from noticing the fascinating sub-groups within a country that are significant to the development of effective evangelistic strategy. Society will be seen as a complex mosaic, to use Donald McGavran's phrase, once we recover from "people blindness." But until we all recover from this kind of blindness, we may confuse the legitimate desire for church or national unity with the illegitimate goal of uniformity. God apparently loves diversity of certain kinds. But in any case this diversity means evangelists have to work harder. The little ethnic and cultural pieces of the complex mosaic that is human society are the very sub-divisions that isolate all Christians from four out of five non-Christians in the world today.

When John Wesley evangelized the miners of England the results were conserved in new worshipping congregations. There probably would never have been a Methodist movement had he not encouraged these lower-class people to meet in their own Christian gatherings, sing their own kind of songs and associate with their own kind of people. Furthermore, note that apart from this E-2 technique, such people would have not been able to win others and expand the Christian movement in this new level of society at such an astonishing rate of speed. The results rocked and permanently changed England. It rocked the existing churches too. Not very many people favored Wesley's contact with the miners. Fewer still agreed that miners should have separate churches!

At this point we may do well to make a clear procedural distinction between E-1 and E-2 evangelism. We have observed that the E-2 sphere begins where the people one has reached are of sufficiently different backgrounds from those of people in existing churches that they need to form their own worshipping congregations in order best to win others of their own kind. John, in Chapter Four, tells us that "many Samaritans from that city believed in Him [Jesus] because of the woman's testimony." Jesus evangelized the woman by working with great sensitivity as an E-2 witness; she turned around and reached others in her town by efficient E-1 communication. Suppose Jesus had told her she had to go and worship with the Jews. Even if she had obeyed him and done so she would have been handicapped in winning others in her city. Jesus may actually have avoided the issue of where to worship and with what distant Christians to associate. That would come up later. Thus the Samaritans who believed the woman's testimony then made the additional step of inviting a Jew to be with them for two days. He still did not try to make them into Jews. He knew he was working at an E-2 distance, and that the fruits could best be conserved (and additional people be won) only if they were allowed to build *their own fellowship of faith.*

A further distinction might be drawn between the kind of cultural differences Jesus was working with in Samaria and the kind of differences resulting from the so-called "generation gap." But it really does not matter in evangelism whether the distance is a cultural, a linguistic or an age difference. No matter what the reason for the difference or the permanence of the difference, or the perceived rightness or wrongness of the difference, the procedural dynamics of E-2 evangelism techniques are quite similar. The E-2 sphere begins whenever it is necessary to found new congregations. In the Philippines we hear of youth founding churches. In Singapore we know of ten recently established youth breakaway congregations. Hopefully, eventually, age-focused congregations will draw closer to existing churches, but as long as there is a generation gap of serious proportions, such specialized fellowships are able to win many more alienated youth by being allowed to function on their own. It is a good place to begin.

Whatever we may decide about the kind of E-2 evangelism that allows people to meet separately who are different due to temporary age differences, the chief factors in the immensity of the cross-cultural task are the much more profound and possibly permanent cultural differences. Here too some will always say that true cross-cultural evangelism is going too far. At this point we must risk being misunderstood in order to be absolutely honest. Throughout the world special evangelistic efforts continue to be made that often break across culture barriers. People from these other cultures are won sometimes one at a time, sometimes in small groups. The problem is not merely in winning them; it is in the cultural obstacles to proper follow-up. Existing churches may cooperate up to a point with evangelistic campaigns, but they do not contemplate allowing the evangelistic organizations to stay long enough to gather these people together in churches of their own. They mistakenly think that being joined to Christ ought to include joining existing churches. Yet if proper E-2 methods were employed, these few converts, who would merely be considered somewhat odd additions to existing congregations, *could* become infusions of new life into new pockets of society where the Church does not now exist at all!

A discussion of the best ways to organize for cross-cultural evangelism is beyond the scope of this paper. It would require a great deal of space to chart the successes and failures of different approaches by churches and by para-church organizations. It may well be that E-2 and E-3 methods are best launched by specialized agencies and societies working loyally and harmoniously with the churches. Here we must focus on the nature of cross-cultural evangelism and its high priority in the face of the immensity of the task.

It is appropriate, now that we have made these distinctions, to stop and see how many people fall into each category. The following table is not an exact tabulation, being in round *millions* of people. It consists, furthermore, merely of a series of educated guesses to illustrate the rough proportions of people around the world who are reachable by various kinds of ministries. The E-0 category is new here. It refers to the kind of evangelism necessary for the "Innermission" of bringing nominal Christians into personal commitment and into "the evangelistic experience." In such activity there is a "zero" cultural distance. There is not even the so-called "stained-glass barrier" that is involved in E-1 evangelism (where one is not dealing with people in the Church but outside the Church and who are yet within the same cultural sphere).

The major point of this table and of this whole paper is that the total

	WESTERN	NON-WESTERN			GRAND TOTAL
		Africa	Asia	Total	
		(In millions)			
I. CHRISTIANS					
A. Committed—Nurture	120	40	40	80	200
B. Nominal—E-O Evangelism	845	76	58	134	979
	965	116	98	214	1179
II. NON-CHRISTIANS					
A. E-1, Ordinary Evangelism	180	82	74	156	336(12%)
B. E-2, E-3, Cross-Cultural Evangelism	147	200	2040	2240	2387(88%)
	327	282	2114	2396	2723
GRAND TOTAL	1292	398	2212	2610	3902

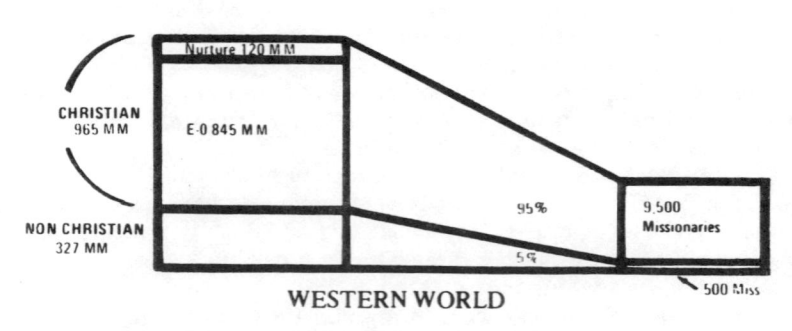

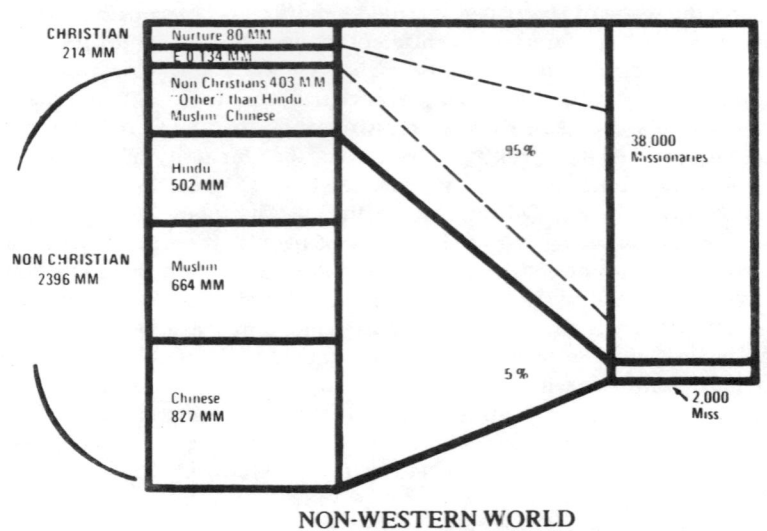

WESTERN WORLD

- CHRISTIAN 965 MM
  - Nurture 120 MM
  - E-0 845 MM
- NON CHRISTIAN 327 MM
  - 95% → 9,500 Missionaries
  - 5% → 500 Miss

NON-WESTERN WORLD

- CHRISTIAN 214 MM
  - Nurture 80 MM
  - E-0 134 MM
- NON CHRISTIAN 2396 MM
  - Non Christians 403 MM "Other" than Hindu, Muslim, Chinese
  - Hindu 502 MM
  - Muslim 664 MM
  - Chinese 827 MM
  - 95% → 38,000 Missionaries
  - 5% → 2,000 Miss

number of non-Christians (2,723 million in the table) are mostly in the E-2, E-3 cross-cultural category. We have spoken of there being "four out of five" who are beyond the reach of the ordinary evangelism of existing Christian churches. These figures make it actually 88%.

The really horrifying fact however is that the worldwide deployment of the active agents of evangelism does not at all correspond to these proportions. One observer has attested that 98 percent of all evangelistic activity in India today is focused on winning nominal Christians, that is, E-0 evangelism, including the work of the missionaries from abroad, while the vast millions of people in the great middle caste and Brahmin groups are virtually by-passed. In other words, the bulk of evangelistic efforts, even missionary activities, are caught up in the internal affairs of the various church movements rather than being focused on even the E-1 category of non-Christians.

The preceding chart utilizes only the Western and non-Western portions from the table above. It also breaks down the 2,396 million non-Western non-Christians into major ethnic-religious blocs, Chinese, Muslims, Hindus, and "Others." This allows us then to make an educated guess as to the deployment of roughly 50,000 Western Protestant missionary personnel. Even if the figures cannot be precise, the over-all picture is clear: the professional missionary today is not in most cases concerned directly with reaching non-Christians, and even if so only a few are focused on the three largest non-Christian blocs in the world today—Hindus, Muslims, Chinese.

Granting that in the long run most cross-cultural evangelists will not be Westerners let us underline the fact that the great bulk of non-Christians will not be reached apart from initial break-throughs that operate along the lines of the traditional and now almost extinct pioneer missionary. Let us look more closely at the great pockets of non-Christians in the world to see why this is true.

One of the great achievements in "mission lands" is the growth of the Presbyterian Church in Pakistan. In a land of 97 percent Muslim it is noteworthy that several hundred thousand former Hindus are now Christian. However a converted Muslim will not feel welcome in the average Presbyterian Church in Pakistan. Centuries-old suspicions on both sides of the Muslim-Hindu fence make it almost impossible for Muslims, even converted Muslims, to be welcomed into the churches of former Hindu peoples. The present Christians of Pakistan (almost all formerly Hindu) have not been at all successful in integrating converted Muslims into their congregations. Furthermore it is not likely to occur to them that Muslims can be converted and form their own separate congregations. The tragedy is that, as a generalization, this kind of impasse postpones serious evangelism along E-2 lines wherever in the world there are any of the 664 million Muslims. However, far to the east of Mecca in certain parts of Indonesia, enough Muslims have become Christians so that they have not been forced one by one to join Christian congregations of another culture. And, far to the west of Mecca in the middle of Africa on some of the islands of Lake Chad, we have reports that a few former Muslims now Christians still pray to Christ five times a day and worship in Christian churches on Friday, the Muslim day of worship. These two isolated examples suggest that Muslims can become Christians without necessarily undergoing serious and arbitrary cultural dislocation. There may be a wide, new open door to the Muslims if we will be as cross-culturally alert as Paul was, who did not require the Greeks to become Jews in order to become acceptable to God.

Vast new realms of opportunity may exist in India too where local prejudice in many cases may forestall effective "near-neighbor," or E-1 evangelism. Indians coming from a greater distance might use E-2 or E-3 methods to escape the local stigmas and establish churches with the 100 or so social classes as yet untouched. It is folly for evangelists to ignore such factors of prejudice whose existence greatly increases the immensity of our task. Prejudice of this kind adds to cultural distance such that E-2 evangelism, where prejudice is deep, is often more difficult than E-3 evangelism. In other words, scholarly well-educated Christians from Nagaland or Kerala might possibly be more successful in reaching middle-class Hindus in South India with the Gospel than Christians from humble classes who have grown up in that area and speak the same language but are stigmatized in local relationships. But who dares to point this out? It is ironic that "national" Christians throughout the non-Western world are increasingly aware that they do not need to be Westernized to be Christian because they cherish for themselves the Christian liberty of self-determination, yet they may in some cases be slow to sense that the challenge of cross-cultural evangelism requires them to allow other people in their own areas to have the same liberty of self-determination in establishing culturally divergent churches of their own.

In any case the opportunities are just as immense as the task. If more than 600 million Muslims await a more enlightened evangelism, there are also 500 million Hindus who face monumental obstacles to becoming Christians other than because of the profound spiritual factors inherent in the Gospel. One observer is convinced that 100 million middle-class Hindus await the opportunity to become Christians but there are no churches for them to join that represent their dietary habits and customs. Is the Kingdom of God meat and drink? To go to the special efforts required by E-2 and E-3 evangelism is not to "let down the standards" and make the Gospel easy. It is to disentangle the irrelevant elements and to make the Gospel clear. Perhaps everyone is not able to do this special kind of work. True many more E-1 evangelists will eventually be necessary to finish the task. But the highest priority in evangelism today is to develop the cross-cultural knowledge and sensitivities involved in E-2 and E-3 evangelism. Where necessary, evangelists from a distance must be called into the task. Nothing must blind us to the immensely important fact that at least four-fifths of the non-Christians in the world today will never have any straightforward opportunity to become Christians unless Christians themselves go more than half way in the specialized tasks of cross-cultural evangelism. Here is our highest priority.

PART TWO:
FOCUS UPON PRACTICE

6.
THE SETTING FOR MAKING CHRISTIANS TODAY

DONALD SOPER

Any consideration of preaching in the light of the contemporary situation must appropriately begin by seeking, from the standpoint of the hearer, what the situation is. There are many respects in which the situation has radically altered and still is changing. We are faced as preachers with a heterogeneity of hearers where once our audience was much more homogenous.

In his day John Wesley had considerable difficulty in appealing to his congregation and was beset with all sorts of problems. A meat chopper wielded by a butcher in Nottingham was the kind of hazard with which he had to deal. As far as I know, however, when he spoke in the open air or indoors, he was not confronted with Buddhist priests. He was not challenged by a Moslem Sufi. In that sense, there is a vast difference between the kind of hearers normally gathering to listen to preachers in this day and generation from the kind of congregation which was accustomed to listen to John Wesley. I remember not so long ago, in the open air, being confronted by a Buddhist priest and discovering early in the proceedings, and not surprisingly, that he knew considerably more about Buddhism than I did. While this is not a common occurrence, to be sure, it does give point to the contention that, when we preach today, we are preaching to people who are likely to contain within their numbers those who have specialized in worlds of which our fathers were simply ignorant. When dealing with the state of the hearer today we are not necessarily confronted with those who know more about the subject than we do. But if we venture outside the realm of pure theology, it is highly likely that at least one member of our congregation will be a specialist in the field in which we are nothing better than tyros.

On the other hand, there is a contrary process, which also limits the kind of group which is prepared to listen to preachers today. There is the selective process whereby the conforming group which is in the habit of listening to preachers does not represent the entire community, but represents at best one or two social, cultural, and class grades in that community. We now know how true it was to regard industrialism as the most lethal drug ever to loosen the ties, and almost to destroy the religious sense itself, of those who became its victims, or its exponents. Though it might be argued that groups within the general industrial complex are still listening to preachers, it is much truer to say that, in general, the industrialized society, at least from the artisan downwards [in economic terms] is almost entirely remote from the words and indifferent to the message of the evangelist.

This problem is further exacerbated by the mobility of human beings today and their dislike of staying in any one place for any length of time. The number of holidays has increased. Nor is it likely in general that when people are on holiday they will receive, or desire to receive, spiritual ministrations. This means that so often our ministry is confined to certain sections of the year, and is also confined to such people as are more or less themselves confined to one particular area. In addition, the disposition of a great many people to move much more frequently than heretofore imposes a strain, because it makes it necessary for the man who preaches to preach spasmodically, as far as his hearer is concerned. Now these are probably superficial areas in which the state of the hearer is regarded, but they are important. But there are other matters which are far more fundamental.

I

The state of the hearer is today mainly secular. The religious background alike for those who go to church and those who stay away from church is largely destroyed. The two regulative factors in the religious background of our fathers was Sunday observance, very largely among those who belonged to the Protestant persuasion, and the Christian year as professed and observed much more largely by the Catholic groups, It is unquestionable that, though there is a disposition today on the part of people in this country and elsewhere to visit churches early on Sunday morning, their attendance is often based on the assumption that they will be required to do nothing more about it for the rest of Sunday. It is also dubious whether they will do anything more about it for the rest of the week.

This is not merely a passing phase. This breakdown of Sunday is a fundamental issue, and constitutes an element in the state of the hearer which is regulative and possessed of great potency either for good or ill. When I was a boy (if you'll pardon the reminiscence), the liturgy of Sunday was not confined to the services. Sunday was a liturgical occasion itself. The whole Sunday for us, in a somewhat Roman and patriarchal and, if you like, narrow-minded household, was given over to a form of ecclesiastical liturgy. We began early in the morning with Sunday school. We then repaired to church. After church we came home to lunch, or to dinner as we then called it, and went back to Sunday school in the afternoon. After Sunday school in the afternoon, we went into the drawing-room for tea. My mother sat at the piano and we sang hymns until it was time to go back to church. We went to church and after church we came home, ate a large supper, and my father said it was a good thing to go to bed early on Sunday. We were packed off to bed, making a virtue of the necessity, because we were "played out" and, had we not been able to go to bed, we should have been compelled to sing more hymns.

Now, my children are inclined to sympathize with me when I tell them this story. I don't ask for their sympathy, and I don't want it. There was a particular value in that kind of liturgial process. It created the rhythm of life—the pulse of life. Once a week our whole attitude to life was first of all authoritatively, and then, more spontaneously transformed. We read what were called religious books on Sunday. We played what was called religious music. And musically we were most grateful for the syncopation of sanctity. We nevertheless were involved in a life for which the regular beat was Christian remembrance. That day has gone. It has not been retained even among those who attend church on Sunday morning, because the value of Sunday in itself has been lost. A secularistic attitude of life as a whole has been put in its place.

For the Protestant, if not for the Catholic, the Christian year has suffered the same eclipse. We now have Mothering Sunday and we shall soon have Fathering Sunday. We have, in the Methodist Church, Christian Citizenship Sunday, and what was "Worn Out Ministers' Sunday" under a more euphonious name, for a Methodist minister may be worn out but nowadays his description is "superannuated." The alteration is best epitomized in the changing of Rogation Sunday which was part of the Christian year, to Farm Sunday, which is a rural ceremony. There can be no doubt whatsoever that this exercise of remembrance, where it is increasingly separated from the pattern of the Christian year, produces a secularism which is almost unavoidable. We may pity our forefathers who slaved in the fields for a mere pittance, but we would do well to remember that they had between fifty or sixty feast days a year when they did not work. Today we have innumerable secular holidays which do not contribute to anything except loss of life on the roads, and some incidental relaxation for some people who otherwise would find little time for leisure.

This is the basis of our secularism. This is the ground for the claim that the passing of Sunday as a day given over to religious exercises, and the neglect of the Christian year, have produced a situation, in which those to whom we preach are not in any suitable condition to receive what we have to say. The pattern and culture and temper and climate of their lives are set in a secular field.

II.

Then there is another phenomenon of which we are all too little aware. It is the difference which exists between the life conscious community in which we now live as compared with the death conscious community in which our fathers lived. I remember as a Sunday school scholar singing a hymn, a tunesome ditty by Sullivan, which reminded me as I sang it of "D'Oyly Carte" in which these words appeared:

> I'm but a stranger here,
> Heaven is my home;
> Earth is a desert drear,
> Heaven is my home.

Another passage in this same hymn goes on like this:

> And time's wild wintry blast
> Soon will be over-passed;

Now those words sound preposterous in our ears. But consult any of the evangelical hymns of fifty years ago, and you will see to what a large extent the emphasis of preaching was concerned with the next world. And it is not difficult to discover why.

Bertrand Russell in his *History of Western Philosophy* points out that up until about the seventeenth century all thinking was about death. It is only by a strenuous effort of will that you and I can think ourselves back into an environment where most people died before they were thirty-five and death was cheek by jowl with the living all the time. People who fell ill probably died of their ailment. In fact, death was the ever-present reality rather than life. Astounding changes have taken place in your lifetime and mine. The expectation of life is now well over sixty. Most diseases are curable and all will be. I remember so distinctly in the "blitz," when I was partly responsible for looking after those who were bombed out in a large area of London, how few people, if any, anticipated that they were going to be killed. Many were killed, but life consciousness even in that disturbing situation was overwhelmingly stronger than the prospect of death. And if you remove the prospect of imminent death, and the close familiarity with it, a new factor enters for the first time in history into the thinking and attitude of ordinary people.

When I began my ministry, I was appointed to a church in the Old Kent Road to the southeast of London, a road mainly famous or notorious for its public houses. One such went by the extraordinary name of "The World Turned Upside Down," and that was an exact description of the place after eleven o'clock on Saturday night. There was great poverty in the district, and one of its simple dramas, and I am speaking of conditions not much more than thirty years ago, was this. When a little child was diagnosed as having TB (in those days it was often called "galloping consumption") she would perhaps go to the hospital, for a time. Then the little one would be brought home, and in one of these dreary, sleazy streets off the Old Kent Road a kind of throne-room would be created in the downstairs parlor facing the street. In the summer time the window would be opened. The bed would be put up beside it and the little one would hold court. People coming by would talk to her and give her presents and watch her die. There was no possibility of a cure, nothing more that could be done. A strangely beautiful though somewhat macabre drama.

But those of my acquaintance who are stricken with this disease today look upon it as a transient inconvenience, and are quite sure that it is curable even in advanced stages. This is a not inappropriate illustration of the difference in the hearer today, who looks upon life with avid hope where once he looked upon death as an ever present possibility as well as an inevitable prospect.

There are the widest repercussions from the change. I remember visiting Jamaica not so long ago and reflecting upon the people who live in that most beautiful island, grandchildren of slaves brought over from the continent of Africa in boats bearing the names of Christian martyrs and captained by Christian skippers who read suitable passages from the Old Testament to the wretches herded like cattle in the holds. As I saw the slums of Kingston, which are all the more horrible because of the sophisticated dirt superimposed upon the primitive squalor of native poverty, I remember that it was out of such experiences of inevitable death that they composed those Negro Spirituals, which we so glibly and easily sing,

> I got shoes, you got shoes,
> All God's children got shoes.
> When I get to heaven gonna put on my shoes
> Gonna walk all over God's heaven.
> But no shoes here, no hope here.
> I got a robe, you got a robe,
> All God's children got robes.
> But when I get to heaven gonna put on my robe.

That expresses the death consciousness of a community which listened respectfully, and sometimes with deep emotion, to the preaching of its time.

Today a slum dweller from Kingston, if he so desires, can quickly cross this delightful island and reach the millionaires' paradise of the north shore—Montego Bay, the haven of rest for the exhausted Hollywood film stars. He may get a job in the kitchen of one of the fabulous hotels. If he does he will see more refuse from the tables thrown away in one night than would be required to feed twenty or thirty families for a week in Kingston. He is not now singing his spirituals about the next world. He is waiting for the Communist agent to arrive to tell him about this one—and I don't blame him.

This life conscious emphasis produces an entirely new reaction. If we talk about eternal life, as under God we are compelled to do when we preach, we must talk about the present possibility which our blessed Lord advocated and himself spoke of. Unless we can outthink, and outspeak, and outlive and, if need be, outdie those who offer life with both hands, we shall make little impact upon those whose consciousness of life and all it offers has been enormously increased even in the few years of our own lifetime.

III.

There is one other great disposing factor in the attitude of the hearer. I am indebted for an introduction to this theme to a very great British Methodist, Dr. J. Ernest Rattenbury, who began his preaching sixty-five years ago. I once asked him if he would tell me what, in his judgment, was the great difference between the attitude of people in his day, sixty-five years ago, and the attitude today. He had no difficulty in answering. He said, "In any congregation, normal or otherwise, sixty-five years ago, you could count on a general sense of guilt. Now the only thing you can count on is a general sense of doubt."

There is a wealth of wisdom in those words. The profound sense of personal guilt has almost disappeared. We are quite ready to impute guilt to others, preferably to groups, but it makes no powerful individual impact. The general attitude if not of doubt, is at least one of curiosity and speculation. This may not be as true of some groups as it is of others. Those who are more fundamentally inclined are more likely to be infused with this sense of guilt even today. But, generally speaking, it is true, and the attitude is likely to spread in the coming days. We have to speak, as preachers, to hearers who are in various stages of doubt.

If we are to deal with the minds and hearts of these doubters we have to begin by recognizing that, partly due to the nature of modern education, and partly due to the spread superficially of forms at least of purported knowledge, there is this almost universal epidemic kind of doubt. Whereas once the processes of education were mainly concerned with pushing into the mind a certain number of nourishing facts, the trend of much education today is the promotion of a kind of critique. It is rather like giving a guidebook on stomachic values to people who are in need of a good square meal. But there can be litle doubt that this process is far advanced, and consequently the mood is not to regard Christianity as craftmanship, but much more to regard it as craftiness. Consequently, before we can make any impression upon those to whom we seek to preach today, we have to recognize that they are already in a resistant frame of mind. They have been encouraged to think very largely in terms of doubt, and the more authoritatively we claim to speak, the more likely we are to produce an ambivalent, if not a contrary, effect to that which we desire. This is the outstanding characteristic of the hearer.

It is, I think, at bottom, a loss of a sense of need. One of the curious effects of preaching today seems to be to stimulate an interest in religion in inverse proportion to the need for it. It is so generally and factitiously assumed that if we can only get people to church, sooner or later, by some kind of inexorable process, they will become Christians. It is my experience that a great many who are brought to church are thereafter inoculated against the real thing and permanently incapacitated for catching it. Without in any way appearing to be contentious, I would beg to remind you that the various evangelical jamborees in our country, promoted a few years ago by a trans-Atlantic organization, produced immediate effects many of which I've no doubt were good. It would be ill advised to denigrate them beyond saying that there is practically no permanent result from them. But, having said that, it is essential to point out that alongside those who were influenced for the good because they were receptive of a totalitarian presentation of "the Bible says," there were a great many people who were so adversely affected that it is almost impossible for any impact to be made upon them by any other kind of Christian evangelism.

That is, if you do not take account of the state of critical dubiety in which your hearer is, you may produce by the very processes of your evangelical, or other kinds of preaching a result which is nothing short of calamitous. Dubiety is not brought to the point of decision because of the loss of the sense of need. No preaching is of effect if it speaks to a situation which does not exist, and proposes a cure for a disease from which the victim is not conscious that he is suffering. Until you can suggest that you have an answer to the problem which vexes the hearer, you have no point of contact with the hearer, you have no attack whereby you can drive home the claim that you seek to make and offer the answer which you believe Christ has. Nevertheless there is alongside this absence of a sense of need an undoubted increase in curiousity.

Our problem is how we can relate this loss of a sense of need to this undoubted increase in a sense of curiosity. Over the last few years there has been an increase of interest in Christianity on the radio and on television, which is in direct contrast to the sense of profound conviction about it. When I first began to speak in the open air thirty-four years ago, people were quite ready to talk about political evils, they were quite ready to talk about the inequities of trans-Atlantic and trans-continental powers, they were perfectly ready to have a go at the parson and to blame the Church, they were quite ready, in fact, to say anything and everything providing you did not endeavor to face them with a religious issue pure and simple. If you did, then they lost interest. It was not their cup of tea. They were not concerned about it. The subject of religion today—not only Christianity but other world religions—has come very much to the fore. One of the "surefire" programs on any television circuit today is a discussion on religion. People will fall over themselves to take part in such discussions and are most anxious to ventilate their own views on such matters. Now this is a fact. In a nutshell, plenty of interest, very little concern.

How are these two matters to be reconciled? The old frontiers and the old bases of thought have largely been eroded and are no longer held with anything like the same consistency. It is this lack of basic ideology which promotes at one and the same time a sense of temporary euphoria and a sense of permanent curiosity. Whereas I can recollect thirty-five years ago the stridency and fervor with which young men professed the Communist case, or others professed the Christian case, or others professed the Socialist case, or others professed the Pacifist case, there has been a gradual withering of these certainties, and in their place has come a wistfulness alongside a sense of personal euphoria. And though it will be untrue to say that we've never had it so good, which was an electioneering slogan very far removed from the truth, it is true that the slogan "I'm all right, Jack," which may also leap across the Atlantic for all I know, is one which expresses this sense of temporary euphoria. It is a reflection of this basic and, I think, utterly constituent element in the state of the hearer.

Whether those who listen today are gathered outside in pagan and nonecclesiastical surroundings or flock inside to early services on Sunday; whether they belong to the various revival groups that are as manifest in the Catholic as in the non-Catholic Churches; whether they are caught up in the revivals of Islam and of Buddhism; or whether they take part in various attempts to resuscitate the Church by adventitious and somewhat unreasonable methods which can be generally regarded as within the gimmick range, yet it is true that these are the elements of a situation which is likely to become further aggravated.

of the hearer is going to be changed quickly. What obviously is required is that we must induce a sense of spiritual values. What is obviously required is that we must re-enforce the sense of spiritual power. And, what above all is required is that we must be able to communicate a sense of true authority. And searching my own conscience and my own experience it would seem to me that the Christian Church, as regards the state of the hearer, is running into more perilous and difficult times than ever. I believe that the city of God remaineth, and I have no ultimate fear. Yet I think the auguries are unfortunate in the sense that the problems are likely to increase and the prevailing mood of secularism and life consciousness and doubt also are likely to increase at least for some long time to come.

7.
WHAT IS THE MATTER WITH PREACHING?
HARRY EMERSON FOSDICK

One might think that such a subject would presuppose preachers as an audience and that an article on it should appear in a magazine devoted to their special interests. On the contrary, there are only about two hundred thousand preachers in the United States, but there are millions who more or less regularly enjoy or endure their ministrations. Whatever, therefore is the matter with preaching is quantitatively far more a concern of laymen than of clergymen. Moreover, if laymen had a clear idea as to the reasons for the futility, dullness, and general ineptitude of so much preaching, they might do something about it. Customers usually have something to say about the quality of goods supplied to them.

Of course, there is no process by which wise and useful discourses can be distilled from unwise and useless personalities, and the ultimate necessity in the ministry, as everywhere else, is sound and intelligent character. "You cannot carve rotten wood," says a Chinese proverb. Every teacher of preaching sometimes feels its truth when he tries to train his students. Whether the grade of intelligence now represented in candidates for the ministry is lower than it used to be cannot easily be determined. As we grow older we tend to idealize the state of things in our youth and to suspect the progressive deterioration of the human race. One theological professor aged seventy, obviously did this when he told his classes that each new generation of students had known less than their predecessors, and that he was curiously hoping to live to see the next one, which he was certain would know nothing.

The best brains today are naturally drawn into occupations other than art, literature, music, education and religion. These spiritual interests are not the crucial and distinctive concerns of our era. We are magnificent in scientific and commercial exploits but mediocre in affairs of the spirit, and one result is the draining of most of our virile minds into scientific invention and money-making. The ministry of religion suffers along with other kindred callings which serve the souls of men with goodness, truth, and beauty. This relative and, I think, temporary inferiority of spiritual callings, however, does not necessarily mean an absolute decline in the intellectual quality of religious leadership; and there is no reason why we should not have much better preaching than we ordinarily get.

One obvious trouble with the mediocre sermon, even when harmless, is that it is uninteresting. It does not matter. It could as well be left unsaid. It produces this effect of emptiness and futility largely because it establishes no connection with the real interests of the congregation. It takes for granted in the minds of the people ways of thinking which are not there, misses the vital concerns which are there, and in consequence uses a method of approach which does not function. It is pathetic to observe the number of preachers who commonly on Sunday speak religious pieces in the pulpit, utterly failing to establish real contact with the thinking or practical interests of their auditors.

Even in the case of a preacher poorly endowed, this state of affairs is unnecessary. No one who has any business to preach at all need preach uninteresting sermons. The fault generally lies, not in the essential quality of the man's mind or character, but in his mistaken methods. He has been wrongly trained or he has blundered into a faulty technic or he never has clearly seen what he should be trying to do in a sermon, and so, having no aim, hits the target only by accident.

No bag of tricks can make a preacher, but if I were to pick out one simple matter of method that would come nearer to making a preacher than any other, it would be the one to which this paper is devoted.

II.

Every sermon should have for its main business the solving of some problem—a vital, important problem, puzzling minds, burdening consciences, distracting lives—and any sermon which thus does tackle a real problem, throw even a little light on it, and help some individuals practically to find their way through it cannot be altogether uninteresting.

This endeavor to help people to solve their spiritual problems is a sermon's only justifiable aim. The point of departure and of constant reference, the reason for preaching the sermon in the first place, and the inspiration for its method of approach and the organization of its material should not be something outside the congregation but inside. Within a paragraph or two after a sermon has started, wide areas of any congregation ought to begin recognizing that the preacher is tackling something of vital concern to them. He is handling a subject they are puzzled about, or a way of living they have dangerously experimented with, or an experience that has bewildered them, or a sin that has come perilously near to wrecking them, or an ideal they have been trying to make real, or a need they have not known how to meet. One way or another, they should see that he is engaged in a serious and practical endeavor to state fairly a problem which actually exists in their lives and then to throw what light on it he can.

Any preacher who even with moderate skill is thus helping folk to solve their real problems is functioning. He never will lack an audience. He may have neither eloquence nor learning, but he is doing the one thing that is a preacher's business. He is delivering the goods that the community has a right to expect from the pulpit as much as it has a right to expect shoes from a cobbler. And if any preacher is not doing this, even though he have at his disposal both erudition and oratory, he is not functioning at all.

Many preachers, for example, indulge habitually in what they call expository sermons. They take a passage from Scripture and, proceeding on the assumption that the people attending church that morning are deeply concerned about what the passage means, they spend their half hour or more on historical exposition of the verse or chapter, ending with some appended practical application to the auditors. Could any procedure be more surely predestined to dullness and futility? Who seriously supposes that, as a matter of fact, one in a hundred of the congregation cares, to start with, what Moses, Isaiah, Paul, or John meant in those special verses, or came to church deeply concerned about it? Nobody else who talks to the public so assumes that the vital interests of the people are located in the meaning of words spoken two thousand years ago. The advertisers of any goods, from a five-foot shelf of classic books to the latest life insurance policy, plunge as directly as possible after contemporary wants, felt needs, actual interests and concerns. Even moving picture producers, if they present an ancient tale, like Tristan and Isolde, are likely to begin with a modern girl reading the story. Somehow or other, every other agency dealing with the public recognizes that contact with the actual life of the auditor is the one place to begin. Only the preacher proceeds still upon the idea that folk come to church desperately anxious to discover what happened to the Jebusites. The result is that folk less and less come to church at all.

This does not mean that the Bible has either lost or lessened its value to the preacher. It means that preachers who pick out texts from the Bible and then proceed to give their historic settings, their logical meaning in the context, their place in the theology of the writer, with a few practical reflections appended, are grossly misusing the Bible. The Scripture is an amazing compendium of experiments in human life under all sorts of conditions, from the desert to cosmopolitan Rome, and with all sorts of theories, from the skepticism of Ecclesiastes to the faith of John. It is incalculably rich in insight and illumination. It has light to shed on all sorts of human problems now and always; and as for the personality of Jesus, if Rodin, the modern sculptor, could feel that Phidias, the Greek sculptor, could never be equalled—"No artist will ever surpass Phidias—for progress exists in the world, but not in art. The greatest of sculptors . . . will remain forever without an equal"—it is surely open to even the most radical of Christians to adore Christ as Master and Lord.

What all the great writers of Scripture, however, were interested in was human living, and the modern preacher who honors them should start with that, should clearly visualize some real need, perplexity, sin, or desire in his auditors, and then should throw on the problem all the light he can find in the Scripture or anywhere else. No matter what one's theory about the Bible is, this is the effective approach to preaching. The Bible is a searchlight, not so much intended to be looked at as to be thrown upon a shadowed spot.

That much insight into contemporary human problems which almost all preachers use in thinking about the practical applications at the end of their sermons might do some good if it were used, instead, at the beginning of their sermons. Let them not end but start with thinking of the auditors' vital needs, and then let the whole sermon be organized around their constructive endeavor to meet those needs.

III.

An increasing number of preachers, too modern by far to use the old, authoritative, textual method which we have just described, do not on that account light on a better one. They turn to what is called topical preaching. They search contemporary life in general and the newspapers in particular for subjects. They discover that in comparison with dry, textual analysis there is such attractive vividness in handling present-day themes, such as divorce, Bolshevism, America's Nicaraguan policy, the new aviation, or the latest book, that they enjoy their own preaching better, and more people come to hear it. It is at least a matter of contemporary and not archeological interest.

The nemesis of such a method, however, is not far off. Most preachers who try it fall ultimately into their own trap. Watch the records of any considerable number of them and see how large a proportion peter out and leave the ministry altogether. Instead of starting with a text, they start with their own ideas on some subject of their choice, but their ideas on that subject may be much farther away from the vital interests of the people than a great text from the Bible. Indeed, the fact that history has thought it worth while to preserve the text for so many centuries would cause a gambling man to venture largely on the text's superior vitality.

Week after week one sees these topical preachers who turn their pulpits into platforms and their sermons into lectures, straining after some new, intriguing subject; and one knows that in private they are straining after some new, intriguing ideas about it. One knows also that no living man can weekly produce first-hand, independent, and valuable judgments on such an array of diverse themes, covering the whole range of human life. And, deeper yet, one who listens to such preaching or reads it knows that the preacher is starting at the wrong end. He is thinking first of his ideas, original or acquired, when he should think first of his people. He is organizing his sermon around the elucidation of his theme, whereas he should organize it around the endeavor to meet his people's need. He is starting with a subject whereas he should start with an object. His one business is with the real problems of these individual people in his congregation. Nothing that he says on any subject, however wise and important, matters much unless it makes at the beginning vital contact with the practical life and daily thinking of the audience.

This idea that we are applying to preaching is simply the project method, which is recognized as the basis of all good modern teaching. The old pedagogy saw on one side the child, as a passive receptacle, and on the other side a subject, like mathematics or geography, waiting to be learned, and, so seeing the situation, proceeded to pour the subject, willy-nilly, into the child. If he resisted, he was punished; if he failed to assimilate it, he was accounted stupid. No good teacher today could tolerate such an idea or method. The question now is why the child should wish to know geography and what practical interest in the child's life can be appealed to in the endeavor to have him desire to know geography. Modern pedagogy starts, not with the subject, but with the child. It adapts what is to be learned to the learner rather than vice versa. Even the food which the child eats for breakfast, coming from the ends of the earth, is used to fascinate his interest in other lands; and we find our children getting at their mathematics by measuring the cubic space of the front parlor or estimating the distance per second which they have walked in an hour.

All this is good sense and good psychology. Everybody else is using it from first-class teachers to first-class advertisers. Why should so many preachers continue in such belated fashion to neglect it? The people often blindly know that there is something the matter with the sermon although they cannot define it. The text was good and the truth was undeniable. The subject was well chosen and well developed but, for all that, nothing happened. The effect was flat. So far as the sermon was concerned, the congregation might as well have stayed at home. It may have been a "beautiful effort," as some kindly woman doubtless told the preacher, but it did no business in human lives. The reason for this can commonly be traced to one cause: the preacher started his sermon at the wrong end. He made it the exposition of a text or the elucidation of a subject instead of a well-planned endeavor to help solve some concrete problems in the individual lives before him. He need not have used any other text or any different materials in his sermon, but if he had defined his object rightly he would have arranged and massed the material differently. He would have gone into his sermon via real interest in his congregation and would have found the whole procedure kindling to himself and to them.

IV.

The meaning of this method can best be seen in some of its corollaries. For one thing, it makes a sermon a cooperative enterprise between the preacher and his congregation. When a man has got hold of a real difficulty in the life and thinking of his people and is trying to meet it he finds himself not so much dogmatically thinking for them as cooperatively thinking with them. His sermon is an endeavor to put himself in their places and help them to think their way through.

The difference in tone and quality which this makes in a sermon is incalculable. Anyone accustomed to hearing preaching must be aware of two diverse effects commonly produced. One type of minister plays "Sir Oracle." He is dogmatic, assertive, uncompromising. He flings out his dicta as though to say to all hearers, Take it or leave it. He has settled the matter concerning which he is speaking and is not asking our opinion; he is telling us. This homiletical dogmatism has its own kind of influence on credulous and impressionable minds. Such minds are numerous, so that such preaching can go on for years ahead. As Jesus said about the Pharisees, such preachers have their reward.

Their method, however, has long since lost its influence over intelligent people, and the future does not belong to it. The future, I think belongs to a type of sermon which can best be described as an adventure in cooperative thinking between the preacher and his congregation. The impression made by such preaching easily is felt by anyone who runs into it. The preacher takes hold of a real problem in our lives and stating it better than we could state it, goes on to deal with it fairly, frankly, helpfully. The result is inevitable: he makes us think. We may agree with him or disagree with him, but we must follow him. He is dealing with something vital to us and so he makes us think with him even though we may have planned a far more somnolent use of sermon time.

Here, too, we are dealing with preaching in terms of good pedagogy. The lecture method of instruction is no longer in the ascendent. To be sure, there are subjects which must be handled by the positive setting forth of information in a lecture, but more and more good teaching is discussional, cooperative. The instructor does not so much think for the students as think with them. From the desire to use some such method in religious instruction has come the forum in modern churches and the questionnaire group after the sermon, where those who wish can put objections and inquiries to the preacher, and discussion groups of all sorts where religious questions are threshed out in mutual conference. The principle behind such methods is psychologically right. We never really get an idea until we have thought it for ourselves.

A good sermon should take this into account. A wise preacher can so build his sermon that it will be, not a dogmatic monologue but a cooperative dialogue in which all sorts of things in the minds of the congregation—objections, questions, doubts, and confirmations—will be brought to the front and fairly dealt with. This requires clairvoyance on the preacher's part as to what the people are thinking, but any man who lacks that has no business to preach anyway.

Recently, in a school chapel, so I am told, the headmaster was only well started on his sermon when a professor mounted the pulpit beside him and offered a criticism of what he was saying. Great excitement reigned. The headmaster answered the objection, but the professor remained in the pulpit, and the sermon that day was a running discussion between the two on a great theme in religion. To say that the boys were interested is to put it mildly.

They never had been so worked up over anything religious before. It turned out afterward that the whole affair had been prearranged. It was an experiment in a new kind of preaching, where one man does not produce a monologue but where diverse and competing points of view are frankly dealt with.

Any preacher without introducing another personality outwardly in the pulpit can utilize the principle involved in this method. If he is to handle helpfully real problems in his congregation, he must utilize it. He must see clearly and state fairly what people other than himself are thinking on the matter in hand. He may often make this so explicit as to begin paragraphs with such phrases as, "But some of you will say," or, "Face frankly with me the opposing view," or, "Some of you have had experiences that seem to contradict what we are saying." Of course, this method, like any other, can be exaggerated and become a mannerism. But something like it is naturally involved in any preaching which tries to help people to think through and live through their problems.

Such preaching when it is well done always possesses an important quality. It is not militant and pugnacious but irenic, kindly, and constructively helpful. How much the churches need such discourses! We have endless sermons of sheer propaganda where preachers set out by hook or crook to put something over on the congregation. We have pugnacious sermons where preachers wage campaigns, attack enemies, assail the citadels of those who disagree, and in general do anything warlike and vehement. But sermons that try to face the people's real problems with them, meet their difficulties, answer their questions, interpret their experiences in sympathetic, wise, and understanding cooperation—what a dearth of them there is!

Yet not only is such preaching the most useful; it is the most interesting. This is the only way I know to achieve excitement without sensationalism. Constructively to state the problem of meeting trouble victoriously, or of living above the mediocre moral level of a modern city, or of believing in God in the face of the world's evil, or of making Christ's principles triumphant against the present international and interracial prejudice is surely not sensationalism, but it is vitally interesting. A breathless auditor came up after one such sermon saying, "I nearly passed out with excitement, for I did not see how you possibly could answer that objection which you raised against your own thought. I supposed you would do it somehow but I could not see how until you did it." There is nothing that people are so interested in as themselves, their own problems, and the way to solve them. The fact is basic. No preaching that neglects it can raise a ripple on a congregation. It is the primary starting point of all successful public speaking, and for once the requirements of practical success and ideal helpfulness coincide. He who really helps folk to understand their own lives and see their way through their spiritual problems is performing one of the most important functions in the modern world.

V.

No method of preaching is without its dangers and, of course, this one which I am espousing has perils in plenty. I presented it once to a group of experienced ministers and collected a galaxy of warnings as to its possible perversions. They thought of times when they had tried it with disappointing results. They had endeavored so precisely to deal with a real problem that Mr. Smith had vexatiously waked up to the fact that they were talking about him, or they had wanted to be so fair about objections to their thought that they had overstated the opposing side and then had neither time nor ability to answer it, or they had been so practical in thinking about some definite problem that they had become trivial and had forgotten to bring the wide sweep of the Gospel's truth to bear in an elevating way on the point at issue, or they had been so anxious to deal with felt needs in the congregation that they forgot to arouse the consciousness of need unfelt but real. All these dangers are present in the method which we are suggesting. It can be offensively personal, argumentatively unconvincing, practically trivial, and narrowed to the conscious needs of mediocre people. But these perversions are the fault of just such unskilled handling as would wreck any method whatsoever.

The best antidote to making a wrong use of the project method in the pulpit is to be discovered in the ideal of creative preaching. The danger involved in starting a sermon with a problem is that the very word problem suggests something to be merely debated and its solution may suggest nothing more than the presentation of a helpful idea to the mind. But we all want something else in a sermon than a discussion even about one of our vital problems, no matter how wise the discussion or how suggestive the conclusion. The best sermons, I still maintain, are preached on the project method but, after all, in the preacher's hands it means something more than the same method in a class-room. It is the project method plus.

What this plus is can easily be seen. When a preacher deals with joy, let us say, he ought to start, not with joy in the fifth century B.C. nor with joy as a subject to be lectured on, but with the concrete difficulties in living joyfully that his people actually experience. He should have in mind from the start their mistaken ideas of joy, their false attempts to get it, the causes of their joylessness, and their general problem of victorious and happy living in the face of life's puzzling and sometimes terrific experiences. This is a real problem for everybody, and the sermon that throws light on it is a real sermon. But that real sermon must do more than discuss joy—it must produce it. All powerful preaching is creative. It actually brings to pass in the lives of the congregation the thing it talks about. So to tackle the problem of joy that the whole congregation goes out more joyful than it came in—that is the mark of a genuine sermon.

Here lies a basic distinction between a sermon and an essay. The outstanding criticism popularly and properly launched against a great deal of our modern, liberal preaching is that though it consists of neat, analytical discourses, pertinent to real problems and often well conceived and well phrased, it does nothing to anybody. Such sermons are not sermons but essays. It is lamentably easy to preach feebly about repentance without making anybody feel like repenting, or to deliver an accomplished discourse on peace without producing any of that valuable article in the auditors. On the other hand, a true preacher is creative. He does more than discuss a subject; he produces the thing itself in the people who hear it. As an English bishop said about Phillips Brooks, "He makes one feel so strong."

Obviously, personal quality is the major factor in producing spiritual power. There is a real reason for the halos which the painters have put about the heads of the saints. They are symbols of something intangible but real—an effluence that ordinary men do not possess, a radiance that is not the less powerful because it is ineffable.

Nevertheless, even a moderately endowed preacher, who never would suggest a halo to anybody, may have some of this power to create what he discusses. Whether he does or not depends a great deal upon whether he sees the objective clearly enough to head for it with precision. If he thinks of his sermon merely as a discussion of somebody's problem he will play with a series of ideas, but if he thinks of his sermon as an endeavor to create something in his congregation he will play on motives. There is where much of our modern preaching fails. The old preachers at their best did know where the major motives were. Fear, love, gratitude, self-preservation, altruism—such springs of human action the old sermons often used with consummate power. To be sure, they sometimes outraged the personalities of both adults and the children by the way they did it but, for all that, they often showed an uncanny insight into the springs of human action. I often think that we modern preachers talk about psychology a great deal more than our predecessors did but use it a great deal less.

One often reads modern sermons with amazement. How do the preachers expect to get anything done in human life with such discourses? They do not come within reaching distance of any powerful motives in man's conduct. They are keyed to argumentation rather than creation. They produce essays, which means that they are chiefly concerned with the elucidation of a theme. If they were producing sermons they would be chiefly concerned with the transformation of personality.

This, however, brings us back to our major issue. If a preacher is to use the project method, as a preacher should, not simply to discuss the real problems of real people but to create in the people the thing that is discussed, his chief interest must be the individuals in his congregation. He must know them through and through, not only their problems but their motives, not only what they are thinking but why they are acting as they do. Preaching becomes thrilling business when it successfully achieves this definite direction and aim. A sermon, then, is an engineering operation by which a chasm is spanned so that spiritual goods on one side are actually transported into personal lives upon the other.

VI.

Throughout this paper we have held up the ideal of preaching as an interesting operation. That is a most important matter, not only to the audience but to the man in the pulpit. The number of fed-up, fatigued, bored preachers is appalling. Preaching has become to them a chore. They have to "get up" a sermon, perhaps two sermons, weekly. They struggle at it. The juice goes out of them as the years pass. They return repeatedly to old subjects and try to whip up enthusiasm over weather-beaten texts and themes. Their discourses sink into formality. They build conventional sermon outlines, fill them in with conventional thoughts, and let it go at that. Where is the zest and thrill with which in their chivalrous youth they started out to be ministers of Christ to the spiritual life of their generation?

Of course, nothing can make preaching easy. At best it means drenching a congregation with one's lifeblood. But while, like all high work, it involves severe concentration, toil and self-expenditure, it can be so exhilarating as to re-create in the preacher the strength it takes from him, as good agriculture replaces the soil it uses. Whenever that phenomenon happens one is sure to find a man predominantly interested in personalities and what goes on inside of them. He has understood people, their problems, troubles, motives, failures, and desires, and in his sermons he has known how to handle their lives so vitally that week after week he has produced real changes. People have habitually come up after the sermon, not to offer some bland compliment, but to say, "How did you know I was facing that problem only this week?" or, "We were discussing that very matter at dinner last night," or, best of all, "I think you would understand my case—may I have a personal interview with you?"

This, I take it, is the final test of a sermon's worth: how many individuals wish to see the preacher alone?

I should despair, therefore of any man's sustained enthusiasm and efficiency in the pulpit if he were not in constant, confidential relationship with individuals. Personal work and preaching are twins. As I watch some preachers swept off their feet by the demands of their own various organizations, falling under the spell of bigness, and rushing from one committee to another to put over some new scheme to enlarge the work or save the world, I do not wonder at the futility which so often besets them. They are doing everything except their chief business, for that lies inside individuals.

If someone utterly "sold" to our American worship of size and our grandiose schemes for saving the world should protest that this means individualistic preaching, he would only reveal his own obtuseness. In one sense, all good preaching and all good public speaking of any kind must be individualistic—it must establish vital contact with individuals. Even if one were speaking on the rings of Saturn one might as well not begin unless one could cook up some reason why the audience should wish to hear about them. The failure to recognize this fact explains why so much of our so-called social preaching falls flat or rouses resentment. A man who on Sunday morning starts in to solve the economic question or the international question as though his people must have come that day of a purpose to hear him do it deserves almost any unpleasant thing that can happen to him. He may be a Ph.D. in psychology but I doubt whether he knows enough about the way men's minds do actually act to be a successful grocer's assistant.

His special business as a Christian preacher with economic and international questions is profound and vital but in so far as he sticks to his last interest as a minister is distinct from anyone else's and it calls for an approach of his own. The world's economic and international situation is not alien to our personal problems. It invades them, shapes them in multitudinous ways; it undoes in us and around us much that the Christian should wish done and it does much that the Christian most should fight against. Let a preacher, therefore, start at the end of the problem, where he belongs. Let him begin with the people in front of him, with what goes on inside of them because social conditions are as they are, with the economic international reasons for many of their unchristian moods, tempers, ideas, and ideals, with their responsibilities and obligations in the matter, and in general with the tremendous stake which personal Christianity has in those powerful social forces which create the climate in which it must either live or die. Such preaching on social questions starts, as it should start, with the individuals immediately concerned, establishes contact with their lives, and has at least some faint chance of doing a real business on Sunday.

Every problem that the preacher faces thus leads back to one basic question: how well does he understand the thoughts and lives of his people? That he should know his Gospel goes without saying, but he may know it ever so well and yet fail to get it within reaching distance of anybody unless he intimately understands people and cares more than he cares for anything else what is happening inside of them. Preaching is wrestling with individuals over questions of life and death, and until that idea of it commands a preacher's mind and method, eloquence will avail him little and theology not at all.

8.
AN OUTLINE OF THE PRINCIPLES OF EVANGELISTIC PREACHING

LAWRENCE L. LACOUR

A. Evangelistic preaching is that form of pulpit address in which the gospel is proclaimed in the power of the Holy Spirit with the intent of eliciting response through an appropriate method.

B. The evangelistic message (See C. H. Dodd, *The Apostolic Preaching and its Developments;* Bryan Green, *The Practice of Evangelism*)
   1. The heart of the evangelistic message: "The New Testament writers draw a clear distinction between preaching *(kerygma)* and teaching *(didache).* Teaching is, in a large majority of cases, ethical instruction. Preaching, on the other hand, is the public proclamation of Christianity to the non-Christian world. For the early Church, then, to preach the Gospel was by no means the same thing as to deliver moral instruction or exhortation. It was by kerygma, says Paul, not by didache, that it pleased God to save men" (Dodd, p. 3).
   2. Both kerygma and didache may be found in pulpit utterances today. Kerygma may be seen as the action of God and didache as the action of man. To a non-Christian audience kerygma logically precedes didache since new birth must always precede Christian action. In evangelistic preaching in America, however, the inability of unregenerate man to achieve didache may become a basic motive for responding to kerygma.

C. The motives for evangelistic preaching
   1. Man's sinful state of alienation from God and man and the evil structure of his environment necessitate the preaching of the Christian message in such a way that men will respond.
   2. God is love. Love cannot be considered an academic affair. In God's love man is judged for being in a state of sin, and in His love man sees hope to which he can respond. Love knows no meaning apart from a love object. Man may respond to the love of God, as seen in the cross, and thereby be saved.
   3. The acts of God—Incarnation, Crucifixion, and Resurrection—become

living events in the evangelistic sermon, thereby eliciting response.
   a. The Word again becomes flesh and springs into life through the personality and the words of the preacher.
   b. The fact of Crucifixion confronts the evangelistic preacher every time he preaches.
      (1) Will he seek response to himself or to Christ? Paul put it, "For we preach not ourselves, but Christ Jesus the Lord; and ourselves your servants for Jesus' sake" (II Cor. 4:5).
      (2) The evangelistic preacher confronts the agony of Gethsemane every time he contemplates extending an evangelistic invitation. Is he willing to offer up himself for the salvation of the people who will be before him?
   c. The power of the Resurrection is at work whenever sin confronts the cross and falls before it. As in the case of the surgeon who defeats death through his knowledge of those factors that make for physical life or death, the power of the Resurrection is present to defeat every evil force that would bring spiritual death to man.
4. Evangelistic preaching flows naturally from the joy of the new life that the preacher experiences in the living Christ. He becomes God's agent seeking the lost coin, the lost son.
5. A basic concept of effective public speaking supports the contention for evangelistic preaching. The late Professor Sarett of Northwestern University used to say, "There are just two reasons why a speaker stands before an audience—either for display, or for response."
6. Our understanding of psychology favors preaching for response through an appropriate method. When one responds to a stimulus by repression—which so often happens when no method of invitation is employed—he has contributed to his inhibitions. When one responds to stimulus through appropriate action, however, the result is a more creative and dynamic personality.
D. The methods of evangelistic preaching
   1. The evangelistic sermon
      a. Usually the most simple and effective evangelistic sermon is the individual witness of what Christ has done. But this personal witness cannot be repeated in good taste each time the minister preaches. This being the case, he must develop a homiletical method for evangelistic preaching. Since the goal of the evangelistic sermon is eliciting response, the preacher should organize his materials according to the usual psychological progression that is followed in response making. (See Alan H. Monroe, *Principles and Types of Speech*.) "These steps are named attention, need, satisfaction, visualization and action" (Monroe, Preface, vii).
      b. Begin by deciding and wording the specific response you seek.
         (1) Low level
            (a) Have an open mind about your spiritual needs.

            (b) Consider the teaching of the gospel that all men need Jesus Christ as Saviour.
        (2) Medium Level
            (a) Decide to become a sincere seeker after the truth of Christ by attending the class that begins this Wednesday night.
            (b) Decide to give the spiritual needs of your life first consideration this coming week.
        (3) High level
            (a) Accept Jesus Christ as your Saviour and declare your intention by signing the decision card.
            (b) Accept Jesus Christ as your Saviour and declare your intention by coming to the altar during the closing hymn.
    c. Further considerations for organizing the materials for an evangelistic sermon.
        1. Try to discover the mental attitude of your audience to the response you seek.
            (a) Types of mental attitude
                (1) Those who believe, yet their beliefs are seldom intense
                (2) Those who doubt, yet their judgment is suspended
                (3) Those who disbelieve and evidence hostility to the ideas of the speaker
        2. Types of belief-making material
            (a) Experience material
                (1) Types
                    a. Direct—"May I share what Jesus Christ means to me?"
                    b. Indirect—"You recall how Masefield pictures the transforming power of God in 'The Everlasting Mercy.'" "In a meeting of Alcoholics Anonymous I heard a man tell this story." etc.
                (2) Tests
                    a. Is it recent? The more recent the more impressive it will be.
                    b. Is it typical? Have such things been happening in the lives of ordinary people? Or is this an exceptional case?
                    c. Intensity—The experiences that come out of the speaker's intense feelings get the greatest response.
            (b) Authority material
                (1) Testimony of experts—The speaker must be an expert in the eyes of the audience.
                (2) Authority of the speaker—An audience is moved to accept a speaker when it is inspired to have confidence in him.
                    a. His basic character

    b. His own personal conviction
   (c) Reasoning material
    (1) Induction
    (2) Deduction
    (3) Generalization
    (4) Argument from analogy
    (5) Cause to effect, effect to cause, effect to effect
  3. Adaptation of materials to your audience
   (a) Believing audience
    (1) Mostly experience material
    (2) Authority material—Use very little.
    (3) Reasoning material is usually omitted.
   (b) Doubtful audience
    (1) Reasoning material—about two-thirds
    (2) Some authority material
    (3) Some experience material
   (c) Disbelieving audience—As important as the development of your ideas will be your own integrity and sincerity.
    (1) Authority material—Don't ngeglect your authority as a speaker.
    (2) Reasoning material
    (3) Experience material
 d. Organize your materials according to the psychological steps in motivation.
  (1) Attention (See Robert T. Oliver, *The Psychology of Persuasive Speech*)
   (a) Methods of inducing attention
    1. Concreteness (Abraham Lincoln)
    2. Conflict (Winston Churchill, Harry Truman)
    3. Finding the unusual in the familiar (F. W. Boreham)
    4. Humor
    5. Variety
    6. The vital
    7. An arresting question
  (2) Need (The effective evangelist in the Eighteenth and Nineteenth Centuries spent no small amount of his time showing his audience their lost condition apart from Christ. Can we not be equally effective in making the word "lost" significant?)
   (a) The meaninglessness of life apart from Christ
   (b) Man's need for values and his inability to achieve them apart from Jesus Christ
   (c) In such crisis situations as illness, financial reverse, and war man sees his utter dependency upon God.
   (d) The roots of anxiety, described psychologically as loneli-

ness and guilt, interpreted theologically as sin and lostness.
(3) Satisfaction
   (a) How does Jesus Christ meet the specific need that has been presented?
(4) Visualization
   (a) Project your listener into the state of a right relationship with God. What changes has he a right to expect?
   (b) Caution: Don't oversell or settle the matter with generalizations. People want to know specifically how Christ can change them. What changes come at the time of decision and what others can be expected to emerge through growth?
(5) Action, or the evangelistic invitation.
   (Following are four basic methods with adaptations)
   (a) The direct appeal to people in the pew
      1. At the conclusion of the sermon ask the audience to bow for a minute of silent prayer. Then ask them to pray for forgiveness, give them Scripture passages of assurance. Finally, request all who wish to be strengthened in their resolve to raise their hands.
      2. At the conclusion of the sermon ask your audience to respond by signing a card or a Response Guide, have the cards passed to the end of the pews, and then request the ushers to collect them and bring them forward for a prayer of dedication.
   (b) The altar call, usually with the audience standing either to sing a hymn of invitation or to remain bowed during soft invitation music on the organ.
      1. An "altar time" may be observed in which every person in the audience is invited to come forward to pray and then return to his pew or to consider himself dismissed. It is better for this kind of altar call to be given to an audience that is seated. Also, the minister should announce that he will be standing at one side of the altar or will be available in a nearby room for counseling.
      2. At the conclusion of the service ask the audience to stand and sing an announced invitation hymn. Then invite those who will accept Christ to come forward and kneel.
      3. This invitation may be varied by asking people to come forward to the altar to stand until the closing prayer when they will retire to a designated room for instruction, counsel, and prayer.
   (c) The invitation to come to a counseling room

1. People may be invited to come directly to the room during the singing of an invitation hymn.
2. People may come in a group from the altar.
   a. Procedures in the inquiry room: group instruction, personal counseling, signing decision cards for records, and prayer.
(d) The "after service," which is held in the same room as the public meeting as soon as those who are leaving have retired and the doors are closed.
1. Procedures
   a. Instruct the group for the number of minutes that you have announced the "after service" would consume.
   b. Give the group a piece of free literature that explains the "how" of your sermon. Be sure to make the offer of this literature a part of the invitation to stay for the after service.
   c. A decision appeal may conclude your instruction period.
(6) Requirements of an evangelistic invitation
  (a) Select the method that will be most helpful for your situation.
  (b) Carefully work out all of the procedures in your own mind from the conclusion of your sermon to the termination of your contact with the last seeker.
  (c) Write out your appeal so that it will be precise and clear.
  (d) Be honest. Let people know each step that will be expected of them before you call for the first step. If you say, "This will be the last verse," stop with that verse.
  (e) You will strengthen your appeal at the close of your sermon and break down resistance if you explain before you start preaching the kind of closing you expect to have for your sermon, and why. If your explanation makes sense to your audience, you can expect little or no opposition. If it doesn't make sense, why do it?
  (f) Be sincere. An evangelistic invitation should be extended in such a way as to help the people and not to save the face of the preacher. Don't let the lack of visible response affect you. Sometimes this happens. But the people have still been given an opportunity to think. End your service on a positive note. Don't "water down" your invitation.
  (g) Be forthright but not coercive. Any method that violates the dignity of the individual violates the basic spirit of Christianity. Dignity is best recognized in the power of free choice. This being the case, an opportunity for choice

must be given, and in the spirit of challenge. The use of pressure cannot be defended upon the grounds that it gets results.

2. Delivering the evangelistic sermon—Maximum effectiveness is achieved by completely writing your sermon and delivering it spontaneously without notes. You may achieve this by:
   a. Reading your manuscript aloud until your message is familiar and felt.
   b. Memorizing the skeleton outline.
   c. Memorizing the key thought in each paragraph. When you can recite the key thoughts in order from the beginning to the end of your sermon and can do so without hesitating, you have your material in hand. Then trust your memory.
   d. Don't memorize your sermon or strain to recall specific sentences just as you have written them. Trust your writing to improve your style of expression, and rely upon memorizing of thought to insure a spontaneous delivery. Quotations or poetry are exceptions. These may be memorized or written on 3 by 5 cards.

3. Preaching with fire—You will speak with conviction if you really believe in what you are saying. If the subject doesn't move you, it will never move your audience. Evangelistic preaching is a personal matter, the proclaiming of truth in which the speaker feels involved. (If anyone thinks he cannot speak with conviction, let him answer how he would speak if he attended a meeting where it had been moved that his salary be reduced a thousand dollars!) You may find the following suggestions helpful at the point of increasing your ability to preach with fire.
   a. Preach from a theme that burns within you for expression.
   b. Live with your completed message until it moves you in its entirety. Keep contemplating the importance of your thesis and hold each idea over the altar of your soul.
   c. Saturate your mind with Scripture on the subject.
   d. Try to have some face-to-face encounter with the specific need that your sermon will attempt to meet.
   e. In your prayer time visualize specific people being changed by the message you propose to bring.
   f. Go into the pulpit fresh from diverting influences.
      (1) Don't accept an invitation to eat out before a service.
      (2) Get at least an hour alone in prayer, not to prepare your message, but to prepare yourself.
      (3) Avoid personal contacts, except on the level of need, before going into the pulpit.
   g. Believe that God is even more interested in the effectiveness of your sermon than you are.
   h. Get up and preach as if everything depended on what you are about to say—it should.

9.
WOULD JESUS STOOP TO CANNED EVANGELISM?

TOM HANKS

Have you, like me, tended to look upon "canned evangelism" with a jaundiced eye? I have often been especially dubious about evangelistic training programs that teach would-be evangelists to memorize a canned approach of presenting the Gospel. This seems so contrary to biblical patterns. Did the men upon whom the Spirit fell at Pentecost need to be enrolled in a course to teach them how to evangelize?

But a gnawing doubt remains. If programs of canned evangelism are to be despised and rejected as unbiblical, why does the Holy Spirit so persistently and abundantly bless the evangelistic movements that employ and advocate such methods? Oughtn't the third person of the Trinity be more discerning in the evangelistic means He employs to bring men to a saving knowledge of Christ? If it were only a question of an occasional exception, we might write it off to the sovereignty of divine grace, or some other convenient theological catch-all for the ways of God that surpass our comprehension.

However, a sober look at evangelistic efforts in recent decades raises at least the suspicion that canned evangelism is well on the road to becoming the norm in evangelical circles. Nobody raised too much of a squawk years ago when thousands of laymen were trained as counselors for the Billy Graham city-wide crusades, memorizing a certain outline and certain key texts of Scripture.

Then in the 1950's Bill Bright began unleashing his Campus Crusade-trained evangelists upon American university campuses and some like myself, who were plodding diligently along in Inter-Varsity groups, threw up our hands in holy horror.

Everybody was being dumped into a common mold! Creativity in the presentation of the Gospel was being stifled! Sensitivities were being trampled upon! Some unbelievers were known to have been offended by stereotyped aggressive tactics. Even whole campuses were known to have become burned over—turned off and unresponsive to the Gospel because of overly aggressive pushing of canned evangelism. We preferred to stick to the frozen variety and couldn't understand why so little interest was generated in our obviously superior packaging.

Meanwhile, in Latin America, the late Ken Strachan and the Latin America Mission were pioneering a strategy called Evangelism in Depth, which involved an effort to mobilize every believer in a given country for house-to-house visitation and presentation of the Gospel to every unbeliever. Again, the Holy Spirit, in His seemingly undiscerning way, blessed in unprecedented fashion. In fact, so unprecedented has been the blessing, that similar movements began to catch fire on other continents—Africa, Asia, and now this year in the U.S. through the effort known as Key 73.

At the Berlin Congress on World Evangelism in 1966, a clash of ideologies became explicit. Dr. Richard Halverson in an important address continued to remind that "Jesus employed a different approach with each person" and "dealt with no two seekers alike." Many Scriptures seemed to make the point quite clear.

The address contained a number of excellent insights, but no attempt was made to explain the Holy Spirit's increasing predilection for the canned approach. Halverson's address was translated into Spanish and circulated in Latin America. I toted copies around and kept asking Evangelism in Depth leaders how we could reconcile Halverson's biblical principles with the experience of the Spirit's blessing on their type of program. Nobody seemed able to give me much help.

A few years later on furlough I found one of our supporting churches involved in the latest wave of canned evangelism—the Coral Ridge brand, developed by Dr. James Kennedy (see his book, *Evangelism Explosion*). Partly motivated by a desire to get a better inside taste of Kennedy's methods I became a trainee along with several struggling laymen of Memorial Presbyterian Church in St. Louis, Mo. (It was not my first exposure to this type of thing. Years previously I had been a counselor for a Graham Crusade and had even submitted myself to a weekend Lay Institute of Campus Crusade.)

This time, since the training included the on-the-job aspect week after week, there was more time for careful evaluation and reflection. I continued to be impressed with the fact that the Holy Spirit did not seem to share my (I thought biblically-based) prejudice.

I saw laymen who at first went out hoping no one would answer the door gradually transformed into mature evangelists who eagerly and sensitively shared the Gospel. I sensed that the Lord was working a change in my own hang-ups and attitudes—particularly in giving me courage to ask direct personal questions about an individual's relationship to God.

Then most unexpectedly one day I saw something in Scripture that had never clicked with me before—Luke's account of Jesus' sending out of the 70. As I pored over the story, our Lord began to look and sound much like Bill Bright or Jim Kennedy.

> After this the Lord appointed seventy others, and sent them on ahead of him, two by two, into every town and place where he

himself was about to come. And he said to them, "The harvest is plentiful, but the laborers are few; pray therefore the Lord of the harvest to send out laborers into his harvest. Go your way; behold, I send you out as lambs in the midst of wolves. Carry no purse, no bag, no sandals; and salute no one on the road. Whatever house you enter, first say, 'Peace be to this house!' And if a son of peace is there, your peace shall rest upon him; but if not, it shall return to you. And remain in the same house, eating and drinking what they provide, for the laborer deserves his wages; do not go from house to house. Whenever you enter a town and they receive you, eat what is set before you; heal the sick in it and say to them, 'The kingdom of God has come near to you.' But whenever you enter a town and they do not receive you, go into its streets and say, 'Even the dust of your town that clings to our feet, we wipe off against you; nevertheless know this, that the kingdom of God has come near.' I tell you, it shall be more tolerable on that day for Sodom than for that town" (Luke 10:1-12; RSV).

You will note that Jesus provides some very definite structure and guidelines for the 70 in their mission. He tells them how to divide up, tells them where to go and what to take (or, more accurately, what *not* to take), what to say, where to stay—even what to do if served unkosher refreshments! Recent studies suggest that passages such as this may have served the early church as training manuals for their own evangelistic efforts. This may be open to question, but isn't it likely that Luke and the early church had some practical reason for preserving such details of Jesus' ministry?

Does this mean then that we are confronted with a contradiction in the Bible—that the Jesus who dealt with no two seekers alike also sent out the 70 with a canned program? No, not if we distinguish between our Lord's example as an *evangelist* and His example as a *trainer of* evangelists. Once I saw this distinction, things began to tumble into place.

It's like teaching someone to paint. In my I-V group we said in effect, "So you want to learn to paint? There's never been a greater painter than Rembrandt. Come with me to the museum and I'll show you some of his masterpieces." The would-be painter is then taken to the museum and taught to admire properly the greatest works of the master painter. Finally we say, "There. Wasn't that inspiring? Now you do it." And afterwards we're frustrated not only because no paintings are produced, but because our pupil doesn't even know which end of the brush to grab hold of!

Programs we have labeled canned evangelism have grasped (at least intuitively) that if you are going to train great numbers of evangelists, you've got to put the cookies on a lower shelf, at least to start with. Unfortunately, at least to my knowledge, they have not made it clear that this is also biblical—that this is the way Jesus worked when faced with the urgent need to train 70 men in a crash program (He was on His way to Jerusalem to be crucified).

Contemporary movements involving canned programs have often been characterized by this biblical sense of urgency—not only to evangelize, but to *train* evangelists—keenly aware that "the harvest is plentiful, but the laborers are few" (Luke 10:2). Is it any wonder that the Holy Spirit has been pleased to bless them?

This is not to say that there are no problems involved. One danger is that of leaving novices boxed into something that ought to be a training program and not a rigid pattern to be mercilessly repeated in all situations. For instance, if after five or ten years a Christian evangelist is capable of nothing more than a mechanical reading of *The Four Spiritual Laws* in every situation, the training has become short-circuited.

I am not convinced that programs of canned evangelism have generally tended to leave trainees utterly boxed into their training program. But on the other hand, such programs have not always encouraged evangelists to develop fully after the pattern of the Master Evangelist who dealt with no two seekers alike.

If you have already experienced the blessing of this training and do find yourself feeling boxed-in to a program that does not adequately fit you for the variety of people you are encountering, it may be time to take your training wheels off. But if you, like me, have felt a certain unyielding prejudice against evangelistic programs, I would encourage you to enroll and get an inside taste. See if your effectiveness as a witness for Christ does not increase—along with new insights into Scripture.

A second danger involves the separation and perhaps even animosity between different groups. I agree that it is unrealistic, and probably undesirable, to think in terms of an official organizational merger between international groups as large as Campus Crusade for Christ and Inter-Varsity Christian Fellowship. However, not only students, but many pastors and church members, will be greatly hampered in their effectiveness if more cross-pollination does not occur.

Often in recent years (both in the U.S. and Latin America) I have been assured by student workers from a variety of organizations that the days of hard feelings and feuding are past. Often the worker will then say that the field is so great and the harvesters so few that they never even see each other (as if to say that ignoring one another was what our Lord meant when He said "love one another"!).

The apostle Paul put it rather bluntly in his first letter to the Corinthians: "The eye cannot say to the hand, 'I have no need of you,' nor again the head to the feet, 'I have no need of you.' " (12:21).

If we can't, and shouldn't, why do we?

10.
THE ART OF COMMUNICATION
BRUCE LARSON

In the days when Yogi Berra was the manager of a baseball team, one of the players was quoted as saying, "Yogi knows more about baseball than all of the team put together. It's too bad he doesn't know how to tell us about it." It is also too bad when committed and knowledgeable Christians don't know how to communicate the central meaning of their own life in Christ in understandable ways to their neighbors, friends, and colleagues.

In Jesus' last appearance to His followers, as reported in the Book of Acts, He said simply, "You shall be my witnesses . . ." (Acts 1:8).

The word "witness" has always scared some Christians. They think of people in unnatural circumstances making peculiar statements and applying pressure on others. But to witness means simply to communicate.

It is true that communication can be illusory. A teacher on the first day of school, explaining the rules and regulations of school life to her kindergarten class, said, "Now, if any of you have to go to the bathroom, raise your hand." A startled youngster in the back row asked, "How will that help?" We make assumptions about what others will understand, and feel certain we're doing an excellent job of communicating, only to find out that we have been thoroughly misunderstood.

The church faces the danger of irrelevancy and non-communication in every age—certainly in our own. The Sunday school, for example, is now undergoing severe criticism and reappraisal. Educators and church leaders in every denomination are discovering that their expensive curricula are often irrelevant and do not speak to youngsters or adults in a language they can understand.

Preaching has come under the same kind of attack. It has often been said that preachers are answering questions nobody is asking. At any rate they too rarely talk about things which have meaning for the man in the pew.

But now let us consider witnessing, not as teachers or preachers, but from the point of view of the layman who is on the frontier of the Church in his daily life.

Recently I have contacted about twenty of the most gifted "communicators" I know, both lay people and clergy. They are men and women who are capable of communicating the truth of the Christian life in natural and relevant ways. Their "secrets" will be found in the following pages.

First of all, what are we charged by our Lord to communicate? Simply the reality and power and love of God as we know it in Jesus Christ, our contemporary. This astounding fact is communicated best relationally, not propositionally. People observe in us the results of our relationship to Christ, and are either intrigued or repelled. Teaching is secondary and usually follows only as people are impelled to ask questions. The old saying, "What you are speaks so loudly that I can't hear what you say," is still true.

Some years ago I was a part of a businessmen's luncheon group in which much of the conversation among the newer men dealt with ideas and theories about God and Christian ethics. One of the men who talked about a relationship to Christ requiring his total commitment often seemed to go unheard. But one day this man left his job, which in those days paid him the magnificent sum of $13,000 a year, to work for a Christian mission paying only a small fraction of that amount. We all knew he had a retarded child who required expensive care. Immediately everything that he had been saying for months as a prosperous businessman took on new meaning. What he *did* communicated far better than all he had previously *said* about the reality and trustworthiness of God.

It has been said that no one is ever argued into the Kingdom of God. Arguments are almost never helpful, but simple answers to life's basic questions, given at the right time, can be a key in the hands of a seeker.

The turning point in the life of Gert Behanna, the author of *The Late Liz*, began when she was invited by a wealthy friend in Connecticut to come and meet some people from her own social set who had had a vital experience with God. She had never met such people before, and got thoroughly drunk in preparation for the ordeal.

As the dinner party progressed, Gert found herself chattering about all of the unfair and unjust things that had been happening to her. Tom and Blanche Page listened quietly. Finally Tom said, "Gert, you certainly have a lot of problems. Why don't you turn them all over to God?" Gert was shocked, and asked, "Do you mean like turning my luggage over to a redcap?" "Exactly!" Tom replied. Some days later, back in her Illinois home, Gert Behanna got on her knees and did just that. It was the beginning of a remarkable conversion.

When are we to be His witnesses or to communicate? Remember that Jesus concluded His final words with the injunction to begin in Jerusalem, the place where the early disciples lived. To us, this means that we are to begin where *we* live, with friends and family and colleagues. This is certainly the most difficult place to witness, but also the most rewarding. The people who know us best are either the most intrigued by our style of life or the most suspicious that what we are does not measure up to what we say. If Jesus Christ has made a difference in us, the people with whom we live and work will know it.

While serving in my first church after my ordination, I met a surgeon who had a great influence on my life. He was the senior vestryman in a local Episcopal church and also part of an ecumenical men's group which met weekly. Most of all, he was a communicator of the love, power, and healing of God in his everyday life. Nurses and interns who worked with him said that he was a perfectionist and "hard as nails," but he prayed before and during every operation and he was able to communicate both verbally and non-verbally the love and power of God to his patients.

One day I asked the doctor when he had become aware of the reality of Jesus Christ. After a long pause, he said, "When I was a boy. My father never made more than forty dollars a week in his whole life, but every Sunday morning in church I saw him put a ten-dollar bill in the collection plate!" This is the kind of communication that profoundly affects our children and all those around us.

Another opportunity for effective communication comes when the person we are with, stranger or friend, expresses a real need or concern. Our response to needs communicates a great deal. If Jesus Christ has begun to meet our own needs, then we communicate verbally or non-verbally to others that we know that He is concerned about particular problems, and that He has answers for them. We don't have the answer, but we can communicate our confidence that God has direction and guidance and is eager to give it.

A government lawyer in Washington, D.C., illustrates how this can take place. Years ago, as a partner in private practice, he began to drink heavily. Before long he became a confirmed alcoholic, and as a result lost his practice and finally his wife. Through an experience of Christ and membership in Alcoholics Anonymous, he began a new life. He was reunited with his wife and rehired by his old firm as a very lowly staff member. As such, he was given a "hopeless" case in which his firm represented one of two large corporations which had been deadlocked in legal proceedings for several years.

One day the lawyer called together the legal advisers for both parties and simply related the story of how God had solved the insoluble problem of his own life. He suggested that most of the men in the room also believed in God, and affirmed his conviction that there was a solution for the very involved problem which was costing both corporations a great deal of time and money. He called for some minutes of quiet in which each man would ask God in his own way what he could do to help solve the problem.

Half an hour later the case was resolved to the satisfaction of both parties. Partly as a result of this incident, a fruitful career in government began for the attorney. God continues to help both individuals and corporations through the guided counsel of this contemporary communicator.

Christians can also find opportunities for witness when someone expresses criticism. Instead of scolding the person for his negative attitude, or sympathizing with him for the apparent injustice, we may be able to ask what he feels he can do to help solve the particular situation or to help the one who is offending him. Because Jesus Christ has helped us with our resentments, jealousies, and criticisms, we can communicate that He has an answer for others.

Two of the most effective communicators I know are men who have inner-city ministries. Bill Milliken works on the Lower East Side of New York City. Bill Iverson ministers to young people in the heart of Newark. Both have identified with minority groups who have much justifiable resentment against society, and particularly against white people. These two white men have identified effectively with non-whites and are challenging them to be part of the answer instead of part of the problem. Our opportunities may not be as dramatic, but they are just as relevant.

Finally, the normal conversations of everyday life are far better opportunities for communication than are contrived situations. The Church has often tried to create times of witness during religious services or other somewhat artificial occasions. My wife and I know a remarkable couple whose lives were changed dramatically during Billy Graham's first crusade in New York. This well-to-do, well-educated, and attractive couple were intrigued by a friend, a fashion model, newly married, who told them in normal conversation about the change that had taken place in her life and in her marriage because of Jesus Christ. This prompted them to go to a Billy Graham meeting, where they themselves began a relationship with Christ.

Returning home full of enthusiasm, they tried inviting their friends in to a weekly Bible study group, but the results were a dismal failure. After many such artificial attempts, they began to learn that it is in the everyday relationships of life that people communicate most effectively, just as their friend had done. These two have since become the center of a whole group of couples who are discovering the reality and power of Jesus Christ.

Certainly there is a time for "visitation campaigns" and for special services in the church. But twentieth-century Christians are discovering, as did their first-century counterparts, that the most effective and relevant communication or witnessing can take place in the market place, at the country club, in the union hall, in the supermarket, and in the office.

Let us consider the actual ways and means of communicating to others. We affirm again that some non-verbal communication must first take place. It is what we do and are, not what we say, that has an impact on people.

Thousands of Americans and even people from other countries know of Ralston Young, recently retired Red Cap 42 at Grand Central Station. This man has discovered authentic communication on the job and has been an example to many of discipleship in our day. His conversations with passengers and his thrice-weekly meetings in an unlighted railroad coach have inspired many of us to put our faith to work.

A Canadian woman confided that several years ago she decided to leave her husband and children and run off with a man who was also leaving his family. They left home and were about to begin a new life under different names. Walking thorough the great concourse of Grand Central Station, where they were to change trains, they happened to look up and see Red Cap 42. They had both heard him speak at a conference some time previously. Just the sight of him was a witness to the Lord whom he served. Turning to her companion, the woman said, "We cannot go through with this. We must return to our families."

Non-verbal communication can be powerful. A layman I know got a call at midnight. A friend of his was drunk and threatening his wife with a gun. The layman rushed over with great fear but with much faith to confront his friend and fellow church member. For two hours he witnessed about his own Christian experience and then he recounted every Bible story that he could recall. He shamed and threatened the man, but all to no avail. Finally, utterly defeated, and frightened that the man might succeed in his attempt to murder his wife and possibly others, he put his arms around his friend's neck and wept. The second man recounted later that it was this loving demonstration which finally got to him. It was not the words but the tears and the concern which convinced him that God cared for him.

But witness at some point must also be verbal. Here are some ingredients I consider important for verbal communication.

(1) *Be intriguing, intelligent, and relevant when you speak about Jesus Christ.* A pious tone or artificial words do not communicate the reality of Christian faith.

(2) *Use the language of the other person.* We must remember that the original Greek of the New Testament was the language of the street, not the language of scholars. Elizabethan English, the language of the King James Bible, is not the language that Americans use today. The truths of the Bible are much greater than any attempt, past or present, to describe them. We must learn to use the language of our day to speak about eternal truths, even as Jesus and the first-century apostles did.

(3) *Be enthusiastic and sincere when you witness.* This certainly cannot be artificially generated. When we are genuinely enthusiastic about who Christ is, what He has done for us, and what He can do for another, effective communication takes place.

(4) *Try to start with a point of agreement.* Even someone hostile to God or the Church will say something with which we can agree. When Harry Emerson Fosdick got into conversation with a man who professed to be an atheist, Fosdick said, "Tell me about the god you don't believe in. Perhaps I don't believe in him either." That was a starting point for relevant communication.

(5) *Express a part of your own needs or of God's answer which somehow touches on the other person's condition.* "Total recall" is unnecessary and will only bore him. Tell that part of your experience that most nearly matches the place where he is struggling right now.

(6) *Ask questions.* This helps the person to talk through his own doubts and fears, as well as his hopes and aspirations. Remember that Jesus was a master in the use of questions.

(7) *Help him to clarify his needs,* to get behind his hurt or jealousy or resentment and tell you what this has triggered in him to make him bitter or depressed at the moment. This enables the person to understand himself and to find a beginning point in his own life where God's answers may apply.

(8) *Don't assume anything.* The person is neither as good nor as bad as he appears to be. Find out what he really believes and feels, and what he wants for his life. One of the best questions might be, "What do you most want to get out of life?" This can disarm even a militant atheist, who may begin to share his aspirations with you. In the same way, don't assume that because someone is a church member he believes all the things his church teaches. By assuming nothing, we let the person speak for himself and clarify his own position in our presence.

(9) *Don't criticize the person for what he is doing or saying.* Try to guide him into some kind of helpful approach that will help him be the person he has told you he wants to be.

(10) *Help him to make a decision.* After he has talked through his problems, hopes, and fears, help him to find a beginning point where he can trust God. It may be an initial decision to turn his life over to Christ, or it may be some next step that will let God take him deeper into the Christian life. Try to pray *with* him, rather than *for* him. Ten words of prayer from him in your hearing will mean more to him than an hour's sermonizing or teaching from you.

(11) *Follow up on this friend frequently in the days that follow.* Have lunch with him, call him, write to him, put him in touch with others if he doesn't live near you. Let him know that God cares and that you care. Encourage him to write to you or to call you often. Let him know that there will be discouragements and setbacks, but that these are normal and he should not fear them.

Finally, let us consider the underlying preparation for communication or witnessing. Since none of us knows at what moment God will give us an opportunity to be His witness, we must always be prepared and on the alert.

First, check your own motives and attitudes. Remember that you are "one beggar telling another beggar where to find bread." This does not glorify you as a witness, but establishes you as one who is witnessing about life and health to another who is also struggling.

Learn to cooperate with the Holy Spirit. Believe that God has been working on each person from the very day of his birth. God can use us to say the "next thing" that someone is ready to hear about himself or God. It is arrogant to assume that we are the first contact he has had with God, and such an assumption can make us superficial and unloving. Let us believe that we are one of God's many agents who will speak and relate to the person's past, present, and future.

Finally, believe in the other person's potential greatness through God. Perhaps this is the most important thing of all. If we believe someone is hopeless, we communicate this. But if, having heard the worst, we believe that God has a plan and an answer for him, even as for us, this too comes across. The person can then take heart and find hope, and be open to hearing whatever we have to say.

Any willing Christian has adequate credentials to be a witness. We need to overcome our self-consciousness and insecurity. To let a sense of inadequacy keep us from being ministers to others is a sin. If someone begins to speak of his needs, believe that God can communicate through some vital thing to help him at that moment.

A bailiff in a Canadian city has discovered God's plan for his life, and he and his wife have had a group meeting in their home for years. One day, with great trepidation, he invited an atomic scientist working on a government project to join the group. The day after the meeting the bailiff sought out the scientist and asked about his reactions. The scientist, who was a bit of an agnostic, had been thrilled by the evening and had found real help, especially in something that had been said by another member of the group, an illiterate Indian.

This is the miracle of God's communicating through His people. The young can speak to the old, and the uneducated to the educated. God wants His people to be witnesses. He calls us to be the individuals through whom He can speak to contemporary man in his deepest needs.

11.

COUNSELING THE SEEKER

CANON BRYAN GREEN

No task is more important or sacred than leading an individual soul into personal conversion. It is a subject which we must approach with the greatest diffidence for the experience of conversion is the work of God's Holy Spirit, and His work as technique; even "principles" is a term which must be carefully used. When we are dealing with real spiritual work we are moving in the realm of God's own working in the lives of men and women, and perhaps all that we are able to say is that we can observe that God normally works along particular lines. We must try to observe how He works and from this observation we can map out certain spiritual principles. Certainly such a careful analysis will reveal to us above everything else that God does move in mysterious ways and that only in utter dependence upon His Spirit can we ever be used to lead a soul to Christ.

This ministry of reconciliation, of leading a soul into a restored relationship with God, is a very personal matter. It is said of D. L. Moody that he was always eager for his sermon to the thousands to come to a close that he might deal with the inquirers one by one in the after-instruction. His instinct was surely right. If some seeker after God then needs help from a Christian in order that he may discover conversion, that task is, for the Christian, one of great privilege, and one which must be undertaken with the utmost care—and, in the best sense, diffidence.

Perhaps it must be emphasized—though no doubt it should be quite unnecessary—that we must keep in the forefront of our minds the fact that each person we are seeking to help is a unique personality and cannot really be classified as a type or member of a class. We may have to group people for the purposes of clear thinking about different types of difficulty or of approach, but we must remind ourselves constantly that no person can be fitted neatly into a pigeon-hole. In any attempt to help him we must seek patience and knowledge, thus making a determined attempt to get alongside him so that he will realize we are friends and are sharing with him, as it were, in his search for conversion.

Individuals will approach the Christian Church for personal help for various reasons. How will the approach be made, and to whom? It may be the result of casual conversation or chance association; it may be made to a parson or to some Christian layman. The essence of the matter is that, however the approach is initiated, the person concerned wants help and is seeking it. To classify the needed help in general terms is exceedingly difficult, but we may perhaps single out four types provided that we bear in mind that the lines cannot be too closely drawn.

There are the many people who turn to the Christian with their human problems—a marriage is breaking up, a parent-child relationship is proving very difficult, a grievance is held against society, there is the inability to find a purpose for life, these problems are real problems and are deeply felt to be such by the person concerned; he must be helped with friendly Christian courtesy. It is our business to put our best endeavor into the attempt to help him to find a satisfactory answer. Every service chaplain or parish priest can amplify such instances from his own experience. It is quite likely that from our standpoint we know that what is really troubling the person is a wrong God relationship and that only when he is right with ultimate Reality will he be able to handle rightly the particular problem; but Christian friendliness and courtesy demand that we do not say to him at the outset: "If only you are right with God then your problem will be on the way to solution." We have been approached with a definite request to deal with a specific problem; our friendliness and attempt to deal with it practically may open up for us in time the opportunity to point out the need for true conversion. If we are watchful we shall discover the possibility of showing that unless the real self is related to God in a living faith the personal life as a whole will not be integrated.

One general warning is needed. We must not feel that we have failed our Lord because people who come to us with their problems often leave us without our having any chance of talking to them about God. We must not get a bad conscience because we have signed five or six forms in a morning and have not said anything about Christ to the people who brought the forms. We are not necessarily being unfaithful servants. In the first place we must never imagine that God cannot use us to draw someone to Himself unless we have spoken the word "God" with our lips. And secondly, we must remember that if we have shown charity and helpfulness this may well pave the way for a future opportunity by creating confidence in the Christian Church which we represent. Given this warning, I think it is true to say that if we are watchful and prayerful we may well discover that with experience we are given the knack—if that is the right word—of being able to get deeper with individuals, and to get deeper more quickly.

There is a second group who come to us—people in search of faith. For one reason or another they have been driven to feel their need for faith in something or in someone, but that is as far as they have travelled. Today this is becoming a more common attitude. The mess and evil of the world and the bankruptcy of science to supply a right spirit with which to handle the situation are driving men to look for a spiritual faith. Many are turning wistfully to the Christian Church because they expect that it may be faith in Christ that they need. They have little or no Christian background; they are very ignorant and do not really know for what they are looking. These people, of course, are not yet ready for conversion, but they are looking for teaching and guidance. What can we do to help such people?

We can lend them a book in order to clear away some of their ignorance about Christianity and to give them an intellectual grasp of the Christian faith. What I have in mind is not so much a pamphlet or tract (useful though these may be in certain instances, they are, generally speaking, too slight for inquirers at this stage); what they need is rather a simply written book on the Christian faith in general, or one giving the answer of Christianity to the particular difficulty that is theirs. It is better both for clergy and laymen who lend books to have eight or nine carefully selected ones which they themselves have read and know thoroughly. Lend the book then, but do not suggest that it should be returned to you by mail. Say rather: "When you have read the book, bring it back to me and I will lend you another." This gives you an opening for your next conversation. You are able to find out what the seeker has discovered and what progress he has made. It is obvious that all of us who are wishing to help others will have different books that we shall lend, but it is worthwhile taking time and trouble to select the books and to prepare ourselves to use them.

Another way of helping a seeker is to suggest certain readings from the Bible, for so great is the modern illiteracy on spiritual matters that many who are seeking God and faith have not the least idea what Jesus Christ actually taught, what He was like as a person, and what He offers to do for men. Do not make the mistake of saying simply, "Read the Bible," or you may discover that your friend starts at the beginning and tries to read right through, as happened once to someone I knew some years ago. Even in such extreme cases, absurd though it may appear on the surface, it is possible—and I have known it to be so—that when the seeker has been desperately in earnest to find God in Christ such a dogged approach to the Bible has been rewarded by the gift of God, for "God is the rewarder of them that diligently seek Him." It is, of course, more reasonable to recommend a straightforward reading of the New Testament. I can recall an American student who came to some lectures I was giving on Basic Christianity in the University of Kansas. After the second lecture he greeted me: "I enjoy listening to you and I am coming to all your lectures, but I don't believe a word you say." Ten days later we happened to meet at breakfast, and this time he greeted me: "Jesus Christ is either mad or else He is God." "What have you been doing?" I asked him, "you have moved a bit since we last met." "Oh, nothing," he replied, "I was interested in what you were saying and so I have read the New Testament through three times." "You will be a Christian soon," I retorted—and he was. These, however, in my opinion are exceptional cases.

Certain Bible passages and books are more suitable than others. In certain circles there is a marked preference for the Gospel of John. I can well understand the love a Christian has for this Gospel. I can well understand the love a Christian has for this Gospel. Archbishop Temple tells us that he himself felt much more at home with John than with any other writer of the New Testament. But I am not convinced that John is the best book for the seeker to read first. It may well be Luke's Gospel that will help him more, and then perhaps parts of the Acts of the Apostles. We must also consider whether it is advisable to recommend that the reading should be in Moffatt's translation or in the Revised Standard Version. It may be useful to recommend an edition of the Bible in which the chapters are laid out as in an ordinary book, without verse divisions. Anything we can do to remove strangeness from the reading of the Bible is valuable. There is no need to put any unnecessary stumbling-blocks in the way of a man who is seeking faith. I have, on occasions, felt it inadvisable to recommend the Bible itself, but rather a Life of Christ which keeps close to the Bible text. It seems to me that at this stage what is required is not so much an exact knowledge of what the Bible says as a clear and accurate outline of the person of Jesus Christ and what He offers to do for men.

Some seekers are guided forward not by reading, but by introduction to a group of fellow-seekers. As in the mission field overseas, so at home it is necessary today that in every parish, clergy or laymen should have a seminar or inquirers' group meeting regularly. Such groups should not meet continuously. Seekers should be gathered together for five or six or perhaps a few more meetings, it being understood that all the members are inquiring the way to faith, and exploring the pathway together. At the end of the period it is usually found that some have passed forward from seeking into faith; others do not at the time wish to pursue their quest; and the remaining few will be helped best by some other treatment.

Yet another method of dealing with the seeker is to invite him to come to church. In very many ways there is no better procedure than this—in fact, I would recommend that as a rule it should accompany any of the previous three methods. I say "as a rule" because there are some people who would be put off by the utter strangeness and unfamiliarity of church worship so that it is best that they should not be asked to come. But for the majority of seekers there is nothing more helpful, provided that the local church is a live, worshipping fellowship. Here he can observe Christians praying and can pray himself, as far as he is able to; here he can catch the atmosphere of worship and begin to realize the impact of the supernatural; here he can listen to God's Word and begin to understand the meaning of the Gospel phrases. So unfamiliar have the ideas of Sion become to so many people that the first step must be to come once more within the sound of such ideas. It is rather similar to a man who cannot understand and appreciate Beethoven. When he begins to go to symphony concerts and tries to listen carefully, gradually he gains some insight into the meaning of the music.

I have outlined four methods of helping the seeker, but there is one principle that underlies them all. We are, it is true, doing our best to clear up his doubts and to answer his questions. We are preparing him for faith, but we must recognize that in a great number of cases intellectual difficulties are not the real cause of unfaith, but are only the rationalization which a man offers to himself and to others of a deeper conflict of tension which has barred him from any vital touch with Reality. The true cause of his lack of faith in God lies in the moral sphere. The Reverend Jack Winslow, speaking out of large experience, categorically states: "There are habits in a man's life which he detests but cannot break, or his conscience is burdened by past sins of which he is ashamed to speak. These things are coming between him and God. Prayer is impossible. God seems utterly remote. Reasons then spring easily to the mind to prove that God has no existence. In such cases no amount of reasoning will bring a man to faith. It is the deeper causes of unbelief which must be tackled." [1]

That is why we must encourage the seeker to make an elementary experiment of faith. "Look at yourself," we may say to him; "if God is real you know what you would like Him to do for you. If there are things in your life which a good God would hate, be willing to let them go. Now pray as best you can. Say to God, 'O God, if you exist, this is what I am like. Help me to find You.' " It is indeed amazing how a glimmer of light is given in response to such an honest self-surrender. In many cases it has been a real step on the way. Fulton Oursler, now a devout Roman Catholic and a writer of many religious best-sellers, tells how, searching for faith and desperate because he could not find it, he slipped into a church and prayed: "In ten minutes or less I may change my mind. I may scoff at all this—and love error again. Pay no attention to me then; for this little time I am in my right mind and heart. This is my best. Take it and forget the rest; and if You are really there, help me." [2] As he prayed the answer began to come. The fact is that many of us who call ourselves Christians do not really believe that God can answer even while a seeker is yet seeking. If a man is willing to give all that he knows about himself to all that he knows up to date about God, then something is sure to happen. How can it be otherwise if we believe what Christ makes plain about the character of God?

The third class of individuals who will come to us for help are Christian people who come for assistance in the Christian life. They are converted, but wish to make progress in sanctification. Here, on the whole, the clergy are better fitted to meet the need and are, in fact, to some extent meeting it. We shall be asked for advice about Bible reading, about church worship, about saying prayers, about overcoming particular temptations, about the positive attitudes that a Christian should take in the secular world, about guidance for life's vocation, and a range of similar problems. There are many good books on pastoralia and it is not my purpose to develop this subject in this chapter. I would, however, like to make these observations. There are beginners in the sanctified life who want help with meditation and prayer. I have found most helpful some advice which Dr. Torrey once gave after a mission he had taken in Cambridge University. He urged the more mature Christians to read the

Bible and pray with a beginner once a week for several months. I took his advice to heart and have often arranged with young converts to meet them individually for fifteen minutes once a week for two or three months. I suggest that we take turns reading a few verses of the Bible together, choosing them from one Epistle, which we read through during the period. The letter to the Philippians is a convenient one for this purpose. After we have read, we each contribute our ideas about the passage and state what help or instruction it gives to us, then we kneel to pray. I begin, turning the words of the scripture into prayer, to make a simple meditation. I encourage the beginner to follow me in his own words. After two or three months I find that the beginner has made real progress in the art of meditation and prayer, and can now stand on his own feet. No doubt many clergy will say they are far too busy to do this, to which I retort: "Well then, you must train your Christian laymen to do it, if you haven't time." And I would add: "It is worth while to make the effort to have fellowship with two or three beginners yourself, for I find that I learn quite as much as I teach."

My other observation concerns the Sacrament of Penance. Christians who come to us for help in many cases are looking for cleansing from sin—not forgiveness in its initial sense of justification, but freedom from a bad conscience which they have as Christians. Here I believe that Catholic experience should guide us, and that the simple, formal method of confession followed by absolution is as valuable a method as can be devised. I know there are some clergy who prefer to get the person to tell his sins privately to God and then to assure him of God's forgiveness. Others suggest an open sharing of the sins, and then together kneeling to seek forgiveness. I have not the least doubt that all these methods are used to bring peace to a Christian's troubled conscience, but there is a great deal to be said for the impersonal and formal method of confession and absolution—at least, for some people and on a particular occasion.

The fourth group who come to us are those who are seeking conversion. They will not, of course, phrase their need like this, but it is what they are seeking. They will probably say, "I want God now," "I want to become a Christian," "How can I find the life that you have been preaching about?" "I want what my friend has got." They are seekers who have pursued the pathway towards Christ a certain distance, and they are ready for something decisive.

These people will come to us on many occasions. Here is a man coming quite casually. From out of the blue he has become aware of his need of God in Christ. Here are our confirmation candidates, for if our confirmation classes have been any good at all that is what many of them should want to know, after the period of instruction. It is the greatest opportunity of all to help young people and adults into conversion. I have often asked communicants about their confirmation preparation, and questioned them as to what the priest asked them during the personal interview. Very rarely did I gather that he asked them in effect, using any phrase he pleased, "Have you found

Christ? Have you discovered a new and living faith in God?" Almost always the question is slanted thus: "Do you understand what I have taught you? Have you made a rule of life? Do you know about the Sacraments?" Look out for other opportunities to lead seekers to conversion. After a mission there will be many; after an ordinary service, if we keep our eyes open; at the time of a marriage, or when visiting in a home.

This group of people who are ready for conversion (if we may describe them as such) are of real importance. In their lives, spiritual processes have been at work through the Holy Spirit; they have moved along the pathway of pilgrimage; they are seeking the decisive moment when their faith in Christ may be certain and real in their experience. Unfortunately, it is just here that so many clergy and lay people "haven't a clue" as to how to help such people. In our theological colleges, hardly any instruction is given in this important art, which we may call the psychology of soul-winning. Very few books have been written about it. A doctor, faced with a patient who needs immediate help, must do something and he must know what to do. The Christian faced with somebody who is at the point where he sincerely and desperately wants God as a living reality in his life must have something to say which will open the door into that experience. It is no good fobbing a seeker off by saying, "Wait, God will come to you if you seek Him. Go on saying your prayers, and perhaps you will discover what you are after." Something more definite must be said, and I do not believe that we ought to stress the waiting. God does not mean, I feel sure, that people should go on and on seeking and never finding. "Seek, and ye shall find," are the words of Jesus.

The Christian minister, therefore, must have some clear idea of the principles which should govern his attempts to lead the seeker into the daylight of conversion. To avoid misunderstanding, I want to make it perfectly clear that many people do come into a crisis conversion without any personal conversation or individual help from a Christian; in fact, there are many who would be hindered rather than helped by such intervention. Their spiritual conversion has been more after the fashion of a bud opening to the sun until the full flow appears. There is something very strengthening to one's own faith in observing men and women coming into the light of the knowledge of God through worship or preaching, through reading or friendship, without any direct and immediate help from another human being.

Nevertheless, there are those who do come to us and say in effect: "I want to come to God, and I want to find Him now." We must remember that at this moment we are touching something most sacred. Here I hope I may be forgiven if I give my own testimony. It is the most humbling experience that I know to lead a soul to Christ, or rather, to be at hand when God finds a soul. Because I have been privileged to be an evangelist in the more technical sense of the word, I have been allowed to kneel beside some hundreds of people at the moment when God broke in to bring the light of His Gospel, yet it is still to me as much a wonder as it was on the first occasion when as a boy of sixteen I was with a friend when Christ came into his life. That was thirty-four years ago, and I am still just as humbled and just as thrilled when I see the knowledge of Christ come into men and women's lives and their eyes light up with joy at the discovery that has become plain to them. It is to me as fresh as ever it was, and completely nothing to do with me. I suppose my own spiritual life has been watered and kept fresh more by such experiences than by anything else—for it is here that I see God in action. If it is not the Holy Spirit of God dealing with the inner depths of their personality, then men may say they understand through the psychology you have used, but there is no light of the joy of understanding in Christ. One knows the difference between speaking that word of spiritual authority which unlocks the gateway of faith and using mere argument which produces only intellectual assent. When, therefore, these privileged moments come I am compelled to stand back and say: "This is the Lord's doing, and marvellous in our eyes." It is for this reason that I covet for every Christian, whether he be one of the clergy or of the laity, that from time to time he may have the privilege of being at hand when God breaks into someone's soul. It freshens, deepens and beautifies with an all-pervading warmth the whole of our ministry. It is something beyond compare with the opportunity of helping somebody in a personal human problem; beyond compare with helping a searcher to go on towards faith; beyond compare with helping a Christian in the life of sanctification. It seems to me akin to the privilege a mother has when she gives birth to her son; new life has come into the world. In the pain and travail of my trying to help a soul, God has given new life; it is spiritual creativeness in its deepest and truest sense which no Christian ought to be denied. I am sure it is God's will for us all, and once we have had the joy of leading a soul to Christ, we shall always be seeking for further opportunities. Because it is the work of God and we recognize it as such, we shall never be in danger of self-glorification. We shall never think that we know how to do it or possess a technique. I hope we shall always tremble when we find ourselves confronted with a seeking soul. What we said so effectively yesterday will not do for today. Unless God gives me the word to speak no real conversion will happen.

What, then, are the principles underlying God's work of conversion? There is one great secret, and perhaps it is the only one. It is to pray for a spiritual sensitiveness which enables one to see how God is leading a soul to Himself and then to seek to be an instrument to lead the soul a little further along the same path. God is trying to disclose Himself; reverently may I suggest that we should ask Him to use us to help forward what He is already doing. Precisely this is the art of soul-winning. Again we are reminded of how completely humbling this fact must always be. We are dependent, utterly so, upon God. We want to cooperate with Him, and He is often willing that we should.

There are a few practical points in dealing with an individual that are quite obvious, but must be mentioned. We shall never help anybody unless we are free from hurry. We must give him quiet, unhurried time. The over-busy parson is a real danger and menace. We should never be too busy to spend time with individuals. It is surely a prior claim in a clergyman's ministry, and I should have said, in the life of any lay Christian. We must give the impression of complete leisureliness when talking with a person who needs our help. He must have our complete interest and attention. A friend once said about William Temple, "he often only gave you twenty minutes, but he gave himself to you for the twenty minutes," and that was why he was able to help so many people, especially younger men and women.

This impression of leisureliness can be created by planning the time carefully. Use some common sense about it. If your visitor arrives at eleven o'clock and you know that you have another engagement at twelve, then you have got an hour for the conversation. Do not start by saying: "We have only got an hour." Say rather, "Now, sit down. There's no hurry; we have got an hour." Then about five minutes before the sixty minutes is up, if there is still more to be said and done, bring this particular talk to a conclusion, thus: "We must stop in five minutes. We have got this clear, or that clear, haven't we? Now when shall we meet again? And in the meantime here are some things that you can do." No doubt I am merely stating a platitude, but it is of the first importance that we should never seem to be pushing people off, or hurrying them in their spiritual pilgrimage.

We ourselves can help by sitting relaxed, avoiding telephone interruptions, preventing others from coming in to disturb our conversation, using for this purpose, perhaps a little "Engaged" notice hanging outside the door. These little courtesies show a considerateness for the person to whom we are talking, and surely are marks of Christian friendliness. Doctors behave like this out of professional etiquette; we surely can do the same out of Christian courtesy.

Once you have sat down for the talk, come to the point quickly. I hope you yourself will be a little self-conscious. I find that I always am when I am alone with one person who is in spiritual need, for the sense of responsibility is great. It is a very delicate affair to go deep down into another person's life that there, in the depths of his being, God may find him. The other person is probably more embarrassed than you are; therefore come to the point quickly. He does not want friendly conversation as an introduction, but to start right away with the business in hand. "Why do you want to be a Christian?" "What makes you want God?" "How long have you wanted to find Christ?" "How have you gone about finding Him?" Questions of this nature are worth asking simply and sympathetically. The real purpose is to find out the background of the individual. Perhaps you have to start a little further back with some such questions as, "What can I do for you?" "Why have you come to see me?" "Tell me what it is you want to know." We shall get all sorts of replies. "My life's all wrong." "I want to be happy as so and so is happy." "I need a faith." "I want religion." We can then develop this a little further by asking, "Have you been to church?" "Were you taught any religion when you were a child?" Or sometimes all we can suggest to open the conversations is quite simply, "Well, tell me about yourself and your life, and any needs and difficulties you feel." The purpose of this introduction is to try to get the person to whom we are talking to interpret himself and to see the way in which God is trying to lead him into conversion.

Perhaps this is a convenient point at which to emphasize one fact which cannot be overemphasized. All the time that we are talking or listening we must ourselves be in a spirit of prayer. Often when silence falls it is a chance to seek God's guidance—an invaluable chance. Sometimes we do not know what to say next; a deadlock seems to have arrived. Be honest. Say something like this: "I don't know what you think, but I feel that neither of us knows what to do next. I don't know what to say to you to help you to understand, but I do know one thing. If you really want God—and certainly God wants you—then He must be willing to show you the way to Himself. Let's take Him at His word and ask Him quite simply to show you the next step. We can do it as we sit here, silently." Such moments of prayer are amazing in their power. Just the right word has often been given to me to speak, or something that I have said before which I now repeat, immediately brings spiritual enlightenment to the friend I am trying to help. In fact, so utterly is this delicate task of soul-winning the work of God's Spirit demanding our complete obedience to Him, that it seems almost impertinent to go on to consider the four main principles underlying the experience of conversion, but go I think we must.

The first principle is that the soul must come to a real sense of need—to the point of despair when it is crying out, "O God I need Thee. Come to me and save me." For it is in the despair of the soul that faith is born. This is what is really meant by conviction of sin. It is when a man discovers that he is lost and helpless, utterly dependent upon God to rescue Him. If there is no answer from Beyond, then nothing can help him. This conviction is much deeper than a mere sense of *sins;* it is rather a sense of *sin,* of *sinnership.* Sins are the fruit of which sin is the root. The Oxford group did much splendid work, but I think sometimes they failed because the regular technique was to suggest that people should make a list of their failures against honesty, purity, unselfishness and love; when the list was made these sins were surrendered. Instead of true conversion, the result was often only a psychological release, because sins had been, as it were, "got off the chest." We must not make the mistake of laying too much emphasis on sins, but rather point out sin for what it really is.

How can we do this? As a start we may well discuss the superficial or surface needs. It may be fear of death or of something else; it may be a deep sense of loneliness; it may be a weakness of will, wanting to do right but failure to achieve; it may be a sense of moral failure, with accompanying shame and guilt; it may be particular sins that are on the mind; it may be a lack of purpose in life, the aimlessness of living; it may be the very evil of the world, with a general sense of frustration and intellectual despair in face of it.

Whatever may be the superficial needs it is our business to show that the real need is for God Himself. The great phrases here are of this kind: "enemy of God, ungodly." "Without strength, away from God." It is the "without God-ness" that is man's real need, and I want to press the point until the seeker realises that he must have God at all costs. It is only out of his despair that he will cry, "Unless Thou help me I must die; O bring Thy free salvation nigh, and take me as I am." We must seek to let God use us as His instrument to bring the soul to the point where it says: "I must have Christ or else I am utterly lost; I am hopeless without Him. Just as I am Lord, take me—take me as I am." So many temporary emotional experiences pass for real conversion just because people are not brought to this point of despair which is real conviction of sin. Never, therefore, hurry at this point of the interview. Far better send a person away again and again with the superficial sense of need unsatisfied until he comes to the crucial point of understanding: "I am without God and without hope. I must have God." Conviction of sin, let me repeat, is conviction of sinnership; it is not just a conviction that one is rather a failure and has given place to some nasty sins in one's life. It is the conviction of a wrong relationship with God, of falling completely short of what man is meant to be. As Archbishop Temple put it: "The alienation of man from God is a fact. It is our business not to deny it but to end it." Our business in soul-winning is to end the alienation, or rather to be God's instrument that He may end the alienation. But first of all the soul must discover the reality of being alienated.

How can the soul discover this? We can explain, simply explain, that the deep need is for God Himself. Point out that it is the "I-ness" of sin over against God; it is the I that rebels against God and won't have God in control. Such an explanation of the mature Christian may seem to be mere words, a merely familiar statement. It is amazing how, if the Holy Spirit is dealing with an individual, such words spoken by the Christian will have a spiritual authority carrying with it the power of conviction.

We can then use the Bible linked with our explanation, but we must know the Bible to be able to use it, and we must believe what the Bible says. The great Bible metaphors about man without God are, "lost," "dead," "blind." If we believe the spiritual diagnosis that the Bible gives we can talk to people like this: The seeker says, "I don't see what you are after." I can reply, "Why should you? You are as blind as a bat—the Bible says so. 'The spirit of evil has blinded the mind of them that believe not.' You must ask God to open your eyes." Or perhaps the opening will be: "I don't feel anything," to which you can reply, "How can you expect a dead person to feel anything? I never knew a corpse that felt anything. The Bible says that you are dead in trespasses and sins." Turn to the Bible passages, point them out, read them together. Then it will happen quite often that the seeker says quite helplessly, "Well, what can I do then? I am hopeless." You immediately reply, "That is exactly what I am trying to tell you—without God you are," and the Bible will have brought, through the Spirit, the conviction of sin.

There is, of course, the other method of using the Bible, by which we point to those passages which tell what the Christian life can be and what God does for those who trust Him. In the seeker's mind there is created a great desire to be what the Bible says he can be and he knows he isn't. But how can he be unless God gives him the power? Here, again, the conviction of sin is beginning to come.

A possible method is that of challenge. It is a combination perhaps of the first two methods, but we should only use it if we find it comes naturally and spontaneously. "Why won't God help me?" asks someone. "Why should He help you at all?" I reply: "Why should He bother about you? You have never bothered about Him." Such a challenge often illuminates the truth, and the seeker discovers that he has no claim upon God and his self-sufficiency is broken down. I remember an undergraduate coming to me and saying that he wanted to be a Christian. We talked for a while about his surface needs, and I said, "Well you are obviously self-centered and superficial. It is a kind of a vicious circle because the more you try to find God the more you concentrate upon yourself and your own efforts. I don't think," I continued, "it's any good talking any more. I can't help you and you certainly can't help yourself, so we had better say goodbye." As I showed him across the room and out of the front door, he kept on protesting that he wanted to find faith and couldn't I help him? As he went out I called after him, "You can't do anything; I can't do anything; but God may be able to do something." When he got home that brought him to his knees in real conviction of sin.

The second principle is to present the offer of Christ to the person who has come to realise his sense of need. This offer is best given from the Gospel story either by some definite passage of Scripture or by some story of how Christ met the need of an individual. Here the particular art is to make the offer of Christ correspond with the superficial need the seeker has admitted. We can show in this way that God meets our need of Him, but that He meets it at the point where we most realise our need. If the superficial trouble was loneliness, let the friendship of Christ meet that; if it was a sense of guilt, then the forgiving love of Christ can bring God's peace. We must never bring the offer of Christ to bear on the person until he has discovered a sense of basic need. Far better send a person away with the words, "I am afraid we can't get any further at the moment. If you don't see that you need God, the offer of Christ will have no meaning." Where there is a realised need, the offer of Christ will become luminous and personal; the soul realises that it is God's answer for himself.

We must not worry about giving a completely balanced presentation of the offer of Christ. At that moment we must not try to present the whole story of Christ's offer. If once a man has come to accept the offer of God in Christ at the point of his conscious need, after his conversion he will realise how much fuller is the complete Gospel offer. Bunyan made that perfectly clear when Pilgrim entered the wicket gate and found the way of life. His conscious need was chiefly how to escape from the City of Destruction; only later did the burden roll off at the tangent of its need; but if the soul gets on the circle of Christ by identification with Him it will not be very long before the soul passes round the whole circle and all the glory of Christ begins to take on meaning.

The third principle is the act of faith. Given a sense of need, confronted with the offer of Christ, the soul must make his reponse. The response is the act of faith—the simple acceptance of what God is offering him in Christ. It is an act of will based upon the truth he is beginning to see. Repentance is the negative side of faith. If I am offered a box of chocolates and my hands are full of stones I drop the stones that I may receive the chocolates. Repentance is the willingness to let drop out of the life all that hinders God that in faith we may receive what God in Christ waits to give. There is no need to stress the idea of penitence and conscious sorrow. This often follows after conversion when the goodness of God and the heinousness of sinning are more truly perceived. If the soul is willing, he can receive the new life in Christ. "The wages of sin is death, but the gift of God is eternal life through Jesus Christ."

We must watch our words carefully. Avoid using the word "do." Faith is the acceptance of a gift God is waiting to bestow. The pride of the human heart is always on the alert to raise its head again by some act of self-effort. Our business is to persuade the soul to cease its deadly doing and simply to receive. A useful illustration is that of a heavily-laden train in the station, with its powerful engine ready to take it on its journey. The coupling link joins together the need of the train and the power of the engine. Faith links my need with God's power. We must not suggest that there is any value or merit in faith. It is simply our trust in God to meet our utter need. "By grace are ye saved through faith."

How can we lead a person into this act of faith? From one point of view we may well ask can there possibly be a way or technique? Surely it is quite sufficient for a soul in desperate need, under deep conviction of sin, to whom Christ has been offered to be told: "Now trust Him," and surely the seeker will come to God as best he can. In fact, may not the act of faith be almost unconscious and be rather an insight that dawns upon the seeker even as Christ is being offered? Will he not grasp at the Gospel as a drowning man grasps at a straw, and believe unto salvation? I am convinced that time and time again this is what does in fact happen and that the eyes of the soul are opened—and we see, believing.

On the other hand, experience shows that many people find it necessary to have a focus for their faith. Personally, I tend to use a passage of scripture—there are many that are suitable. For example, we can turn to: "Come unto Me, all ye that labour and are heavy laden, and I will give you rest." "How much more shall your Heavenly Father give the Holy Spirit to them that ask Him?" "Him that cometh to Me I will in no wise cast out." "Behold I stand at the door and knock; if any man hear my voice and open the door I will come in,"—and many others. Consider one method of using,

"Behold I stand at the door and knock; if any man hear my voice and open the door I will come in." I like to point to the passage in my New Testament and then explain its message. God takes the initiative and approaches the soul in its need. Hearing His voice means, as a little girl once explained, "to feel wrong inside and as if you want Jesus." The opening of the door is the act of the will which trusts God in Christ to take control. "Suppose," I suggest, "I own a room, but keep it filthily dirty and untidy, with broken furniture about the place; supposing you love me and knock at the door, offering to enter and help put things straight. How would I let you in? Surely I should say, 'Come in, please; turn out the broken furniture and help me tidy up.' So with Christ; ask Him to enter your life; say to Him, 'I am yours. Come in, turn out the broken furniture of bad habits, take away the pictures and put up on the walls of my imagination pictures of Christian standards; clear up the dust and sweep away the filth.' That is what the act of faith in Christ means. That is how we open the door." I then go on to explain very carefully that Christ has promised to come, if we will open the door and receive Him. And faith rests on His promise and not on our feelings.

What happens next? There is a good deal to be said for sending the seeker away to do his own business alone with God. This is not a time for any other person to obtrude. There is, however, a practical difficulty. For many people there is not the opportunity to be quiet and alone. Besides, our Lord made it so clear in His parable of the sower that "when the seed is sown then cometh the devil." The pressures of the secular and the material are tremendous, and the still small voice can be so easily drowned by the noises of daily life. That is why it is often wiser to suggest that the seeker should make his response of faith to Christ immediately and in another's presence. If this is what I decide to be best I say, "Let's kneel down together that you may put your trust in Christ." It is very rarely that I ask the seeker to pray out loud. I want him to forget me at this sacred moment and to talk to God alone. Rather do I tell him that I want him to be alone with God and to open his life to Christ. I simply say, "Just tell me when you have finished praying. Then we are silent. I pray while he is praying. After a while he indicates that he has finished praying. Immediately I ask, "Has Christ really come to you?" or, "Has God made Himself real to you?" or, "Has He met your need?" If it is the work of the Holy Spirit and a real act of faith has been made, the answer is almost invariably something like, "Yes, I think so." My next question is equally important: "How do you know?" As I have tried to explain so carefully a few moments before that we must trust the promise of Christ and that it is not any feelings but what Christ says that matters, one would expect the answer to be something like, "Because Christ promised to come." Invariably the answer is quite different, on these lines, "Because I feel it," or "I know it." In other words it is an experience that has come, an inward realisation of Christ's presence that has been given. I always answer, "I am glad to hear it, Thank Him out loud." The instant response is a simple act of witness in a few words of thanksgiving. The simple words are very often only, "Thank you,

Lord Jesus, for coming to me." At this point I pray. I do not say: "Lord, I thank Thee that he has let Thee into his life and that Thou hast become his Saviour and Lord. Please show him what to do next and help him to read the Bible, to say his prayers and to go to church; help him to make resolutions against sin and to become a full member of the Church." That would be laying down rules and regulations at the very moment when grace has acted in response to faith. No, the kind of prayer that will help at this stage is something very simple: "Lord, I thank You that You have come into his life and become his Saviour and Friend. Help him to keep his eyes open to see what You tell him to do next, that he may know that You are leading him and may learn to trust You better. Amen." The act of faith must pass into the attitude of faith. "As many as are led by the Spirit of God, they are the sons of God."

There is the fourth and last principle of which we must take note. We are meant to have the certainty of assurance. In the New Testament we are offered not only a personal relationship with God in Christ, but the certainty of that personal relationship whereby we can cry with confidence, "Abba, Father." This assurance is not concerned with our feelings or passing emotion. It is a conviction of faith based upon the very character of God. Saving faith is not saying as it were, "Please God come into my life." It is saying, "Thank you, God, because you have come." We must point out to the new convert that we are not asking him to believe in a few words printed in ink on a piece of India paper. Behind those words, "If any man hear my voice and open the door I will come in," stands the whole act of God in Christ which guarantees His character, guarantees that He is a God who has come to deliver. We must point out something of the meaning of the death of Christ on the Cross—Christ, who gave Himself for people who did not want Him and tried to put Him out of their lives upon a cross. Behind those words, "I will come in," stands the Person who said them—God in Christ, Who pledges Himself in the death on the Cross to give Himself to all sinners who will receive Him.

In this way we try to insure that the new convert's faith rests on God and on His character alone. We do not need a faith which rests on anything more than the character of God, and if it rests on anything less it will not suffice. It must rest where only it should rest—in God himself. Human pride has been broken and the new convert can take no pride in his feelings, no pride in a resolution, no pride in a changed life. He is trusting in a promise, and it is impossible to have pride in a promise which is based on the character of somebody else's love. His experience is in fact, "Nothing in my hand I bring; simply to Thy Cross I cling."

There is one final point that I must make quite clear. I am not suggesting for a moment that the procedure I have outlined, with its four principles, is a pattern slavishly to be followed. God deals with the human soul in a variety of ways. All that I am trying to emphasise is simply that when we analyse the movements of a soul in conversion, these four principles seem to operate. I have separated them out for the purpose of clear analysis, but in the actual event they may not be clearly defined. I have no intention of stereotyping the approach of God to an individual and that individual's response to God's approach; and this applies both to the gradual, almost unconscious conversion as well as to the crisis conversion which we have been specially considering. It applies equally to the man who comes into conversion by himself through some unexpected means, and to the man who seeks out help from a Christian.

In this chapter we have been considering what we are to say to a seeker who comes to us desiring to find God. We tried to show him his need and put before him the offer of Christ. He leaves us believing in God, in God Himself—in God because of what He is. His conversion and his assurance are anchored in the love of God and in nothing less. This is the object of all soul-winning.

Note on Repentance

The biblical context sees the individual as a person in-a-relationship. He is a person in relationship with sinful humanity, of which he is inescapably part. He is saved into the Body of Christ when he finds himself a person in right relationship with God and his fellows. God deals with us as sons, that is, as differentiated personalities, but He does not deal with us in isolation from our fellows.

It is for this reason that the barrier to faith at the time of conversion is often an unwillingness to get right with our fellows. It is not, of course, that *by* putting ourselves right with others we are therefore putting ourselves right with God, or, worse still, can think that we can earn His forgiveness; it is rather that, because an individual is a person inescapably in relationship with others, he must be willing to be in right relationship with others—which is the only real situation for him. Thus only can he find himself in a position to be put right with God—Who is Reality.

This basic idea should guide us when dealing with the seeker at the point when he is ready to make an act of faith. It may well be that he finds he cannot accept the offer of Christ because of a barrier. This barrier may turn out to be an unwillingness to put right some wrong human relationship. We must not say to him, "You cannot make an act of faith and accept Christ as Saviour and Lord until you have put yourself right with your fellow." Rather we should say: "If you are willing to straighten out the relationship, then that is what God wants at this moment." This is important because repentance is not a change of mind which puts us right so much as a change of mind which makes us willing to be put right. To alter the wrong human relationship at this moment may well seem to the seeker to be beyond his power. If, however, he is willing to be put right he can then make the act of faith, and discover Christ as Saviour. After his conversion the power of the new life will enable him to alter the relationship which he is willing should be altered.

We need not list such wrong relationships. A few illustrations will be sufficient. A young woman seeking Christ could find no peace and assurance. The barrier was a theft she had committed in a house where she was working. "It's five miles off," she cried, "and it's too late to go tonight." I pointed out that God wanted at that moment her willingness to restore the stolen property, not the act of restoration. She was willing, and immediately able to believe. Next day, in the power of her conversion she was able to make the restitution.

I remember a man alienated from and antagonistic to the Christian Church because of his contact with a certain group of Christians. He wanted Christ, but was unwilling to accept the fact that after his conversion he would still not be perfect, just as the Church herself is not perfect, he was able to discover the peace of God, and shortly afterwards to find his place within the Christian Church.

A middle-aged woman on the point of conversion suddenly said: "But I won't forgive my sister; for twenty-five years we haven't spoken." Until she was willing to forgive, God's forgiveness could not be given to her. But it is important to notice, "Until she was willing," and not, until she felt forgiving.

This same principle is important when dealing, for instance, with alcoholics. The barrier to faith in their case is often the sense of utter impotence to get rid of the habit. How, then, can they become true Christians? Only when they see that by letting themselves go to Christ as they are, willing to be delivered, can Christ come to them. After their conversion the power to overcome the habit will be theirs.

---

[1] J. C. Winslow, *Reaching the Nine-Tenths:* p. 8.
[2] Fulton Oursler, *Guideposts:* September, 1950.

12.
LET'S MARCH ABREAST: THE CONGREGATION IN EVANGELISM

GEORGE E. SWEAZEY

The congregation is God's intended evangelistic agency. That is why He put the church on earth. Most of those who through the years have been brought into the Christian life have come in across the growing edge of a local church. Each church is a mission station surrounded by people who are missing what God sent His Son to earth to give them.

Most church members know this well enough. When Christians see the spiritual need of those without Christ they zealously want to do something to help them to know the wonders of the new life in Jesus Christ. Unfortunately, most church members do not know what to do about it. In any meeting where evangelism is discussed, they will talk endlessly about the sort of evangelism they do not believe in. But if the chairman says, "Let's talk about what we can be doing," a great silence falls upon the room. This chapter will deal specifically with what can be done—that which is spiritually valid and possible in any church. "For you hold in your hands the very word of life" (Phil. 1:16, Phillips).

THE COMMITTEE

Evangelism is the church's most urgent, but unfortunately, sometimes its least pressing, task. It can always be postponed. A minister is never finished in his work with those already in the church. Attending to the Lord's "other sheep that are not of this fold" is easily put off until some "free time" becomes available—a time that never seems to come. Lay workers, too, are under unremitting pressure to complete the tasks immediately at hand— preparing for the canvass, getting teachers for the church school, and so forth. Doing something about evangelism is postponed from month to month, from year to year, even from decade to decade. Because evangelism can be so easily neglected, the work must be anchored firmly within the structure of a congregation by the appointment of a committee that will submit regular reports to the church board. Then something is likely to happen.

A layman should be chairman of this committee. The minister may well be the coach of the evangelism team, but it will function best with a lay captain.

A lay enthusiast will usually push the minister and everybody else. The committee may be a very few persons in a small church, or up to thirty members in a large one. It should have enough members to be in contact with most of the church organizations and activities. *Evangelism is not a special activity for special people at special times; it is a normal activity for all church people all the time.* Whether it is realized or not, every activity of the church can be directed in such a way that will help to reach the goals of an evangelism program.

Remember this, for it is of great importance: *No one person is the evangelist.* The evangelist is not the special speaker at mass meetings, or the warm-hearted Christian who asks about your soul, or the pastor of the church. Every person in the whole Christian fellowship, should be an evangelist. In the fourth century, Jerome said, "Baptism ordains the laity." When the layman was baptized, he was ordained to evangelize. If his church does not show him how to do it and give him opportunities, it has cheated him of a function God demands of him.

Seeing evangelism as the work of the whole church helps avoid the old suspicion of arrogance—"You ought to be like I am," or the manipulation—"Do what I say and you'll get right." Evangelism is not one person working on another person; it is God working through the fellowship on each person involved in it. The plea of evangelists is simply, "Come where these great things are happening!"

This chapter will show that evangelism encompasses a wide range of activities that take a great deal of time. For two thousand years Christians have been seaching for a quick and easy method of evangelism. It will never be found. Nothing so great can be simple. But when the whole church is the evangelist, no one has too much to do. The evangelism committee can help provide opportunities for each member to contribute to the program.

Let us think of the committee at its first meeting. Imagine that it is trying to get a program of evangelism started in its church. Its first concern must be the congregation. All members are needed to make contacts with people outside the church, to draw newcomers into church participation, to reveal the beauty of the Christian faith, and to help new members get a sound start in the church and in Christian living. It can be assumed at the beginning that many members will have small interest in this. They may recoil from the word *evangelism*; they may shun interference with other people's religion, or lack of it; they may not want to "spoil a fine congregation" by bringing in strangers who might not be congenial. These attitudes are not consistent with Christianity, so they must be erased. Members can develop an eagerness to bring people into the church. It comes from gratitude, faith that is worth sharing, a deep concern for people, and the habit of looking for people to reach. These new attitudes must be laid upon the hearts of the church people in sermons, prayers, classes, and group discussions. The alert committee tries to plan for this.

The committee needs to determine clearly what it hopes will happen to people. What sort of person should evangelism try to produce? Is the goal to make "nice people"? To aim souls toward heaven? To radicalize people and separate them from an exploitive culture? Bringing people into a saving relationship with Jesus Christ may do everything necessary. "If anyone is in Christ, he is a new creation" (II Cor. 5:17*). The committee might describe a person in Christ as a person:

*References are to the Revised Standard Version unless otherwise indicated.

(1) Who believes that God sent Christ to live, and teach, and die, and rise again to reveal His saving love for man. This truth will be the organizing center of that one's cosmology, anthropology, philosophy, and politics. It will illuminate his understanding of himself every minute of the day.

(2) Who has Jesus Christ, not just as a one-time Savior, but as an always-present friend and helper.

(3) Whose life is so dominated by love for God and people that he is joyfully open to others of all sorts, ready to listen, to trust, to care, and to share their joy and sorrow. This will affect relationships at home and at work, in every social contact.

(4) Who is blazingly intolerant of all that blights and corrupts human life, of misery and injustice, and is therefore dedicated to the struggle against these by every means God gives.

(5) Who is eagerly learning more of God's truth from the Bible and the history of Christian experience.

(6) Whose conduct is governed by the love of Christ.

(7) Who is a consistent, growing, and strength-giving member of the church.

Without such a well-defined goal as a measure and guide for an evangelism program, its total "product" can too easily become the mumbling of some misunderstood responses and a new card in the church member file. We must realize that the great result can be only God's doing, but He commands His church to provide the circumstances. The committee has to ask whether the essential thing will be happening to those the church attracts. Will it happen in church services, or classes, or conversations, or by reading? Will it be radiated through the fellowship or caught from Christian friends? Will it perhaps come through joining in some effort to help people? A transformation of the church program might come from asking such questions. However, if a church is not organized to reveal Christ to newcomers, it will be no more than a religious racket for the members it already has.

THE FILE OF PROSPECTIVE MEMBERS

Evangelistic invitations cannot be addressed, "To whom it may concern." There is no such person. Of the many needy people near your church, the only ones it will reach are those you have identified by name and face. The listing of these is the start of all evangelism. There are only four pieces of furniture that a church really needs. It can do without hymnals and pews, but it must have a Bible, a Communion table, furnishings for baptisms, and a file of prospective members. That last is not anticlimax. The whole evangelistic field of the church should be in that file. Rarely will anyone be won whose name has not been listed there. The amount of evangelism will depend on how well that list is kept up. It will have four sections: "Not Yet Seen"; "For Cultivation"; "For Decision"; "Very Difficult."

The list is built by hard work from many sources:

(1) *Church school parents.* Many who think the church has nothing for them will, nevertheless, send their children. These people can be drawn closer through church school P.T.A. activities. Also, a church school enlargement program may well have parents in mind.

(2) *Visitors to church services.* In a small church, alert officers can get their names. A large church has to ask all attenders to register in order to get the names of visitors. Those who greet at the door can get addresses by asking, "May we send you news about the church?"

(3) *Participants in church activities.* Church clubs and classes try hard to attract outsiders as a first stage in evangelism. Their members are urged to bring new people. Special programs are planned for this purpose. Fishers of men use bait. A club for young married people has special evangelistic opportunities. A church should have specific procedures for getting the names of club visitors and church school parents into the evangelism field.

(4) *Church member contacts.* The friendship of church members with those outside the church is the greatest source of evangelistic outreach. Members must be urged not merely to submit names, but to give the first invitations themselves, and to report the result.

(5) *Less useful sources.* A neighborhood religious census is likely to be a waste of time because it is so easy to take but so hard to use. It should never be taken unless specific plans have already been made to follow up the contacts it makes. Members can check Welcome Wagon lists, new utility connections, and new public school enrollments. Such sources have some use, but they are far less useful than the contacts the church can make for itself.

The results of every approach and all relevant data are recorded in the file; cards should also include recommendations. No card is ever taken from the file for any purpose until it is permanently removed.

PROGRESS

When a contact has been made, what then? Very few people, except those who have recently left another congregation, will be ready for church membership. If, by some charmed persuasion, newcomers could be brought at once into church membership, it would be a disaster for them and for the church. It has been argued that, in order to hold people, we should get them at once into the church where they will spend the rest of their lives learning what they need to know. The difficulty is that a stream does not rise above its source. If people start with a low estimate of what a Christian is, or what church membership requires, they are likely to remain there—if they remain at all. The required faith and vows are very simple, but also very searching. People should have some idea what the words mean when they say, "I accept Jesus Christ as my Lord and Savior" or, "I will strive to be a faithful member of the church."

An evangelism program must have long-range methods of preparing people for membership. It should try to get newcomers into the worship services, fellowship groups, classes, Koinonia groups, and social action task forces. It has to trust that in these will be found the strange, radical, world-shaking, world-forsaking, loving, and glorious reality of Christianity. The church can also provide books and pamphlets to provide the truth at various intellectual levels.

The approach may start with a phone call, which does no more than show a friendly interest—"Glad you were in church" or, "We heard you moved to this area." These calls find out whether there is any use in further contacts. Where there is, home calls are needed. These try to arouse interest in various sorts of church participation, and bring back recommendations for future steps. A letter can prepare for personal approaches, but by itself it does little good. The postman cannot do the churchman's work, but the church can do much to arouse interest. Having children in choirs brings nonmembers to church services. Ushers and greeters can help make a church attractive. Coffee and punch after services give a chance for meeting visitors and making them want to return. It helps if the building looks loved. Church organizations need an officer who receives in writing the names of those who might be interested, with a card for reporting what he does about the opportunity and the result. Here again, mailed invitations do little good except as preparation, and the telephone is inadequate. A concerned "Let me stop by for you" or, "I'll be looking for you at the door," is all that really works. Consider such questions as: Does the church have enough doors? Will one visit encourage a second look? Other entrance points are groups for young adults, for parent training, for community action, for prayers, or serious reading.

COMMITMENT

When the newcomer has had an opportunity to learn about the Christian faith and life, and the meaning of church membership, and to feel the beauty and the splendor of it, then the question must be raised, "Is this for you?" Decisions are important. Psychology joins theology in holding that it makes a world of difference when people definitely make up their minds and say so. The Christian life cannot be a matter of "I suppose so" or, "Perhaps." The Bible again and again calls for commitment. Jesus said, "Every one who acknowledges me before men, I also will acknowledge before my Father who is in heaven" (Matt. 10:32). Paul said, "If you confess with your lips that Jesus is Lord, and believe in your heart that God raised him from the dead, you will be saved" (Rom. 10:9). Most of our days pass in uneventfulness, but there are some that tower up like mountain peaks. From them we get our bearings. It is the business of the church to bring such days. A life-governing decision needs to be expressed in words, and there needs to be some sign that puts it in the realm of tangible reality. Joining the church is such a sign.

The purpose of evangelism is not to bolster an institution. That temptation is always there, for we like to have a going concern. We do want to have the church, the body of Christ, present on as many scenes as possible. We want it to be a strong instrument for Him to use. But we also believe that God put His church on earth to give blessings that every human being needs. We want Christians in the church because we believe they need it. A religion whose key word is *love* requires fellowship.

There are countless circumstances in which a decision for the Christian faith may be expressed. The opportunity may present itself at a church service, a youth retreat, a communicants' class, in the pastor's study, or during a conversation in a home.

EVANGELISTIC CALLING

There are great advantages in having religious decisions made in homes. The most intimate questions are thus faced in the familiar surroundings, where a person can be most at ease. There will more likely be a sharing of thoughts with a caller whose coming shows he cares. A lay caller demonstrates the friendly interest of the members, whereas a minister is paid to make calls; his point of view is professional. "A jury discounts a paid witness," but a layman tells what his faith and his church mean to him from the layman's point of view. Also, only members have available the great number of hours evangelistic calls require. What is more, great benefits come to the callers. An evangelist must always be his own first convert.

Evangelistic visiting is not connected with any particular theology or era. It has always been important in the church, and always will be. It is equally useful for staid or "swinging" congregations, for pietists or activists. It is simply an ideal method of communicating whatever a church has to say.

Depending on the motives of the people involved, it can be perfunctory or searching, manipulative or respectful, a smooth technique or an experience of how great it is when people get beyond superficialities and open up their hearts to each other.

If a church does not have many experienced callers, there are great advantages in arranging a program over several evenings in a row. If dates are made far enough ahead, it is as easy to engage callers for successive evenings as for scattered ones. New callers who are uncertain the first night can gain confidence on succeeding ones. The group can learn by discussing the calls of the night before. If there is supper and a meeting before the visiting, members can concentrate on training which progresses from one night to the next. A guest trainer can be engaged if the minister of the church wants a fresh voice.

Does this talk of "training" suggest learning how to empower people? It is not that at all, but one must realize that callers can make mistakes if they have not considered them in advance. Contacts may expose sensitive areas, and there are possibilities of harm as well as good. The essential qualifications are faith and a love of people, but those will not save the caller who cannot think how to get a serious conversation started, or finds himself losing out to the television set. A voluble witness must learn to listen. Similar situations keep presenting themselves, and callers can profit from what others have learned across the years. We could make fun of the idea of a manual for visitors, as though the teacher could run his thumb down an index and find a pat answer for every question. But callers must give information and remove misconceptions. When someone says, "We don't think we should join the church until we know how long we will be here" or, "I would have become a church member long ago, but there is something in the Apostles' Creed I don't believe," the visitor should not have to improvise and answer as though such a response had never been heard before.

The visitors know that these are not just social calls. They are praying for decisions that will bring measureless blessings in all the years ahead. Imposing a purpose may well intimidate them. They may find it almost impossible to raise the significant questions they have come to ask. Without help, many callers will never get beyond saying, "We've got the best choir in town; don't you want to join our church?"

If it is not possible to go calling on successive evenings, or if a sufficient number of opportunities are not evident, a Sunday afternoon and evening, or a weekday evening, may be best. New callers may go out with those who have had experience. Even experienced callers should have some preparation—no one ever knows enough. The veterans need to renew their humility at the greatness of the task. Simply to hand out assignments and send the callers on their way is to arrange for failure. What they are trying to achieve is something only God can do. They need a strong sense of His presence and His help. Many a person who is asked to make such calls replies, "That's not in my line; I'm just not cut out for that sort of thing." They are quite right. But if they try it anyway, they are likely to come back declaring it has been one of the greatest experiences of their lives. In this they have had a clear proof of the miraculous.

The committee will need one of the books or booklets on how to arrange a calling program. This will explain how to enlist callers, give suggestions for their instruction, and tell how assignments are made.

Jesus "called . . . the twelve, and began to send them out two by two (Mark 6:7). The two-by-two plan is still best. More than two may seem overpowering, but a lone visitor is not as impressive as two, and he needs a helper. Some churches have a permanent calling organization—"The St. Andrew's Fellowship," or "The Seventy." How often callers go out depends upon how often the list can be renewed. To have only a few calling programs a year works better for new member classes, but this may cause people who are ready to be seen to wait too long.

There are three different kinds of evangelical calls:

(1) Prospect calls show welcome, stir interest in particular church activities, and get information. Attractive personalities are important, but no special skills or knowledge are needed by the callers.

(2) Decision calls are made to those who may be ready to make decisions for Christian faith and church membership. These callers must be qualified, spiritually and intellectually.

(3) New member calls are made to welcome new members and to help them get a good start in the church.

GIVING A GOOD START

The most important part of evangelism comes after the decision has been made. No evangelistic decision was ever good enough. If the decision is supposed to mean birth into the new life in Christ, then one would have to say of all of them, "I don't believe in it." The decision can be of great importance. It can be the definite facing in a new direction, the finally saying Yes to Christ, and meaning it. But one of the church's most damaging mistakes is thinking that this moment of decision marks the entrance into the Christian fold. The most able preacher, the most dedicated caller, cannot, in the little time available, let people know just what it is they are deciding. The pressing need is to put content into the decision. Here are some of the next things to be done:

(1) *Minister's interview.* When callers come back with joyful news of positive response to the gospel, the minister needs to make an appointment to talk with prospective members. He wants to take them farther in their understanding of what their decisions mean; he must become their pastor and their friend.

(2) *New member class.* A class gives an incomparable opportunity for instructing, inspiring, and motivating at the time in life when these will mean the most. Prospective members are usually eager to know more about the Christian faith and life, about the church and its history, about practices, attitudes, and duties, and about the life of the local church. Class sessions offer one of the best ways of validating a decision. They may change the minds of some who thought they were ready to join the church. Some churches require attendance at such classes. There need be no worry about making it too difficult to join the church—people want what is obviously important. It is strange when a boy has to do more to become a Tenderfoot Scout than an adult has to do to become a member of Christ's church. The new member class may serve as an inquirers' group for those who are still undecided. Written materials will be needed. In small churches the classes may have just one or two members—but this has advantages.

(3) *Youth communicant class.* Joining the church can be a momentous event for boys and girls. In preparing for it they will think more deeply and do more class work; they are also more easily reached emotionally than at any other time. A church which considers business-as-usual in the church school to be all the preparation needed for such a decision, throws away a priceless opportunity. In the past two decades the tendency has been for the number of such classes to increase to include people from ages six to forty, or even older. In this matter, other churches are coming to where the Lutherans have always been. Every boy or girl with whom the church has contact should at some time be asked to consider a profession of faith and joining the church. The age at which this should be presented, and the method of doing it, need to be determined. It can be done in a church school class, a youth group, a special service, or in a personal interview. Letters to the homes can ask for the parents' prayers and interest in this. We must be aware of the danger of making it appear that joining the church is an automatic next step for those who reach a certain age or complete the class. It must be a deeply felt personal decision, without group pressure. Near the end of the course of study there may be private conferences at which each pupil can talk with a minister or church officer about this great step, and whether or not to take it.

(4) *Literature.* Much that the new members need to know can be given them in books or pamphlets. This material should not be handed out all at once. With each piece there should be a personal word about why it is important.

(5) *Written Forms.* Those who join the church are asked to make the most profound statements the human mind can encompass, and the most binding vows. Therefore there must be a chance to think and pray about these in advance. That is why many churches have them printed on forms

which can be pondered, and then signed. These same forms may have spaces for biographical information the church needs, such as a record of baptism and past church experiences, and a check list of services that can be offered to the church. A sheet may explain, step-by-step, how one joins the church. New members may be given membership certificates.

(6) *Joining.* Getting married and joining the church are the greatest occasions in any life. Both should be arranged so that they will be remembered ever after with gratitude and joy. When joining a church is perfunctory and hasty, to suit the convenience of officers or the minister, it is a travesty on the church and a dishonoring of the Holy Spirit. A great deal of thought should be given to ways of making this occasion solemn, impressive, and joyful. For example, a church officer may be assigned to sit with each new member and family. Those who are joining are presented, not just by name, but with some friendly personal details. There may be a welcoming talk with good advice. Representatives may describe various church activities and invite participation. Pledge cards may be presented and stewardship explained. Perhaps each new member could sign a historic covenant or roll book. There may be a tour of the church building. You may wish to take a group picture, and later post it so the new members can be identified. New members may be assigned to duties or task forces. They may make a statement of their faith and purposes. Then, as the church of Christ, you may wish to celebrate the Lord's Supper together. A social reception might be the last event.

At the public welcome before the congregation, there should be a sense of celebration. The new members may be called forward to answer questions about their faith and purposes, or to make statements in their own words. The congregation can pledge its love and care. The minister, in behalf of the congregation, may give new members the right hand of fellowship. Flowers or pins may be given the new members so they can be recognized and greeted afterwards. The minister may stand in the church aisle throughout this ceremony so the new and old members face each other. You may wish to have them stand at the door so other members can greet them on the way out. Certainly the lay officers could take much of the leadership in this ceremony.

No one church would do all these things. However, they are listed to suggest different ways small or large churches can make joining memorable.

(7) *Fellowship.* The natural laws of social life are against incoming members. They think of the church as someone else's club into which they must not thrust themselves. And the love of Christians has a seamy side which makes the old members enjoy each other so much they have no time for newcomers. Unless church members work against these tendencies, new members may never make good friends in their new church. Likable extroverts do well enough, but many people need a great deal of help.

Here, as with prospective members, group activities and classes have a big part to play. They receive the names of all new members and set their enrollment processes into operation, not counting on the mail or telephone, but making personal engagements for the first meetings. The committee's budget may provide guest tickets for dinner meetings.

(8) *Sponsors.* Everybody's business is nobody's, and the congregation's promise of "our Christian love and care," will die with the shaking of hands unless someone is designated to carry it out. Assigned sponsors should make calls or extend newcomers invitations to their homes. They can arrange to meet their new members at the church and introduce them to others. However, this plan works well only when someone sponsors the sponsors. If there are neighborhood parish divisions, the parish leaders may be the sponsors.

(9) *Pledges.* Getting the new members' pledges is important, not because the church is eager for their money, but because it is eager for their hearts, and Jesus' saying is still true, "Where your treasure is, there will your heart be also" (Matt. 6:21). Those who have a weak financial relationship with a church are likely to be hard to hold and hard to please. New members need guidance. If they are expected to guess how much the pledge should be, the guess may be a poor one. Stewardship methods and motives can be explained in the new member class, at the time of joining, by house calls, and in writing. The first pledge sets the level for the future, and it should not be delayed.

(10) *Service.* Members never really feel that "their church" is "my church" until some of their lives are built into it through giving their time and effort. New members are reluctant to check a list for how to offer their services, unless they are prompted. Churches must avoid the danger that the record for proffered services will be left in a file, with the new members feeling rejected because they were not asked for what they offered to do. Sometimes certain regular services are reserved for new members—such as leading the responsive reading, delivering flowers to the ill, helping in the financial canvass.

(11) *Status Check.* The list of all who have joined during the past two or three years should be checked regularly to locate any who are getting a weak start. This situation may be remedied if it is caught soon enough, but before long it becomes incurable.

The saddest duty in any church is the removal, from the roll, of the names of those who can no longer be considered active members. When this is done the mood is likely to be critical—"They were poor members" or, "They did not keep their promises." If those under criticism were on hand to answer, as they usually are not, they might reply, "The church did not keep its promises to us. Where was all that friendship and help we heard about? We were left to sink or swim, so we sank." The ultimate success or failure of evangelism depends most on what is done *after* people join the church.

FOR THE CHURCH

Karl Barth said that when a church quits evangelizing "it begins to smell of the 'sacred,' to play the priest and mumble. Anyone with a keen nose will smell it and find it dreadful." A congregation turned in upon itself tends to become stiff and cold and formal. Reaching out to others is the surest source of new life in a church. It forces a church to think of what its essential purposes are, and of how well it is achieving them. "For their sake I consecrate myself" (John 17:19). The power of the Holy Spirit is not given to those who, with folded hands, are looking up to heaven, waiting for a visitation. It is given to those whose hands have taken up a work for God that is impossible without His help. The effort to make the Christian faith plain for others is what best makes it clear for the members of a church. "Evangelize or fossilize" is still the law.

It is beneficial if these answers to the question, "What can we do about evangelism?' have made it seem a large task. The unchanging rule is, *Shortcuts in evangelism never work.* Only a congregation whose gratitude, love for God, and love for man impel it to carry through the whole long process, will ever have, or deserve to have, the great reward. That reward is to see people and homes radiant with the wonder and the beauty of the love of Jesus Christ.